NEW MEXICO!

NEW

UNIVERSITY OF NEW MEXICO PRESS
ALBUQUERQUE

SECOND REVISED,
ENLARGED EDITION

MEXICO!

Marc Simmons

For Liz

*Second revised,
enlarged edition*
(*New Mexico!* was first
published in 1983 by
Gibbs M. Smith Inc.,
Peregrine Smith Books,
Salt Lake City).
Original ISBN:
0–87905–135–3

TEACHERS:

A comprehensive Teacher/
Student Guide is provided
with each class set of this
textbook. If you do not have
the Guide with your class
set, please request one by
writing on school letterhead
to the publisher:

University of New Mexico
Press, Order Department
1720 Lomas Blvd. NE
Albuquerque, NM 87131-1591

CONTENTS

MAPS AND CHARTS

TO THE STUDENT

We are about to go exploring. We will travel across mountains and deserts. We will also travel far back in time. In this book we will explore New Mexico—yesterday and today.

History is a window to the past. Studying history lets us see what happened long ago. It shows us that we are part of the long flow of human events. New Mexico's history reads like an adventure story. That story is filled with exciting events. It tells of people, good and bad. It tells of times, happy and sad. By learning about these things, we can better understand ourselves. In that way, we become better citizens.

New Mexico is a land of three dominant cultures. Culture is everything created by people. Culture is a people's way of living. It is beliefs, customs, language, and all the things we make and use. A song is part of culture. So is a car or a TV set. A baseball game is a part of culture, too. Culture includes religion, law, education, and all the rules we live by. Together, the many pieces of our daily lives make up our culture.

Different peoples have different cultures. Each has its own way of doing things. When two cultures come together, one is usually stronger than the other. Conflict often follows. In the end, the stronger culture wins over the weaker. But something new is formed. The two cultures blend together. Each culture has learned from the other.

What are New Mexico's three dominant cultures? The first was the Indian culture. It is the oldest. Thousands of years ago, the Indians of New Mexico developed their way of life.

Later, the Spaniards brought another culture. It was the culture of Spain. The Spaniards arrived on horses. They carried guns and a cross. They conquered New Mexico

culture

and their culture became the common way of life. In 1998 New Mexico marked its 400th birthday. People remembered much that had happened to New Mexico since the Spanish settled here in 1598.

Still later, a third culture was brought to New Mexico. We call it the American or Anglo culture. It came with people from the eastern United States. They conquered the land once more. They introduced new traditions and customs.

New Mexico's three dominant cultures—Indian, Spanish, and Anglo—helped shape the way we live today. But other peoples and cultures contributed, too. Blacks, Asians, Middle Easterners, and many people of other countries have settled in New Mexico. Each added to our New Mexico culture. All three dominant cultures changed because of this blending.

In this book, we will follow New Mexico's story through time—from the ancient Indian hunters to today's space scientists. When you finish the story, you should understand better why New Mexico is called "The Land of Enchantment."

NEW MEXICO!

New Mexico's Topography

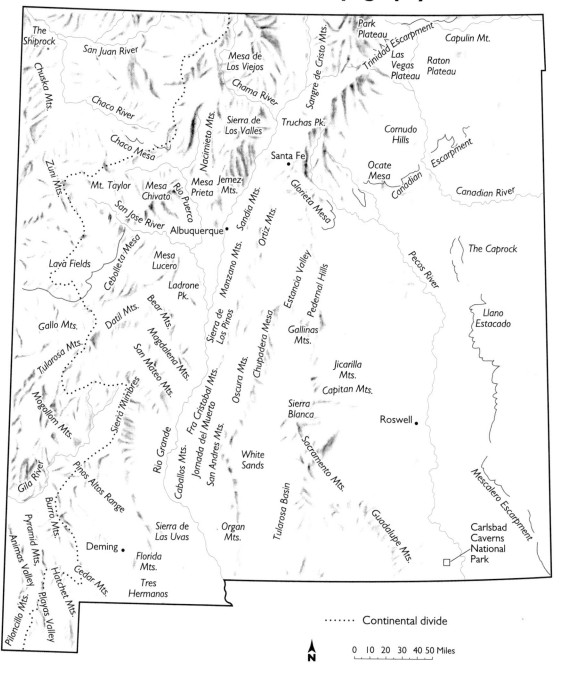

The Shiprock

San Juan River

Chuska Mts.

Chaco River

Chaco Mesa

Nacimieto Mts.

Mesa de Los Viejos

Chama River

Sierra de Los Valles

Park Plateau

Trinidad Escarpment

Capulin Mt.

Las Vegas Plateau

Raton Plateau

Sangre de Cristo Mts.

Truchas Pk.

Cornudo Hills

Escarpment

Zuni Mts.

Mt. Taylor

Mesa Chivato

Rio Puerco

Mesa Prieta

Jemez Mts.

Santa Fe

Ocate Mesa

Canadian

Canadian River

Sandia Mts.

Glorieta Mesa

San Jose River

Albuquerque

Ortiz Mts.

Pecos River

The Caprock

Lava Fields

Cebolleta Mesa

Mesa Lucero

Manzano Mts.

Estancia Valley

Pedernal Hills

Llano Estacado

Ladrone Pk.

Gallo Mts.

Datil Mts.

Bear Mts.

Sierra de Los Pinos

Chupadera Mesa

Gallinas Mts.

Tularosa Mts.

Magdalena Mts.

San Mateo Mts.

Oscura Mts.

Jicarilla Mts.

Mogollom Mts.

Sierra Wimbres

Rio Grande

Fra Cristobal Mts.

Capitan Mts.

Sierra Blanca

Roswell

Gila River

Pinos Altos Range

Caballos Mts.

Jornada del Muerto

San Andres Mts.

White Sands

Sacramento Mts.

Mescalero Escarpment

Burro Mts.

Sierra de Las Uvas

Organ Mts.

Tularosa Basin

Guadalupe Mts.

Carlsbad Caverns National Park

Pyramid Mts.

Deming

Florida Mts.

Animas Valley

Hatchet Mts.

Cedar Mts.

Tres Hermanos

Piloncillo Mts.

Playas Valley

········ Continental divide

N

0 10 20 30 40 50 Miles

1

THE
LAND

The land we live on helps form our culture. It has helped shape our history. To understand the people of New Mexico, we must understand our land. New Mexico is special because the land is different from any other place. Here we begin our study of this special place.

New Mexico is a beautiful and sunny land. Tall mountains seem to touch the sky. Plains are wide as the sea. Deserts shine in the clear air. Rivers and lakes sparkle in the sun. New Mexico is a good place to live and grow up.

New Mexico is in the part of the United States called the Southwest. Look at a map.

New Mexico's Location

You will see that New Mexico is **bordered** on the east by Texas. A small part of Oklahoma touches New Mexico on the east, too. To the north is the state of Colorado. To the west is Arizona. The Republic of Mexico borders part of New Mexico on the south.

New Mexico is one of the Four Corners states. Corners of New Mexico, Colorado, Utah, and Arizona all touch at one point. That is the only place in the United States where four states meet.

bordered

Look at the map again. New Mexico is almost square shaped, but not quite. In the southwest corner, a piece of the state juts into Mexico. That piece of land is sometimes called New Mexico's Boot Heel.

The Continental Divide crosses New Mexico from north to south. It is a ridge running down the western side of the state. This ridge divides the flow of waters. On the east side of the Continental Divide all waters flow toward the Atlantic Coast. On the west side, they all flow toward the Pacific.

Geography

To understand the history of New Mexico, we must first understand our state's geography. Geography is a study of the land, plants, and animals. In other words, geography is the study of the environment. Everything in nature around us forms part of the environment.

People are part of the environment, too. Our place in nature is important. We can use the environment wisely. Or we can cause it great harm. History shows us the problems people have had when they did not use the environment wisely.

Long ago, New Mexico looked very different. The land as we know it today had not yet taken shape. For millions of years, forces inside the earth were shaping the land. High

geography
environment

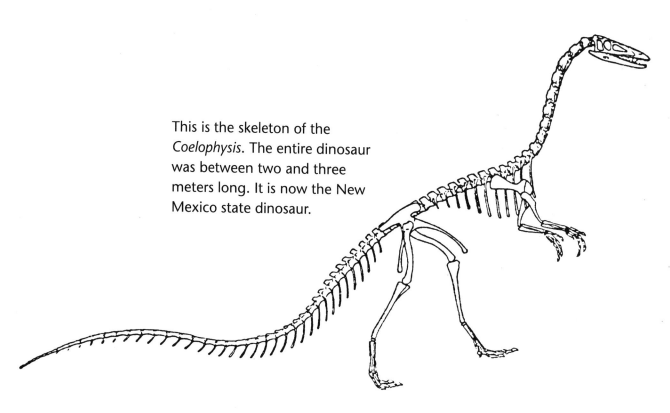

This is the skeleton of the *Coelophysis*. The entire dinosaur was between two and three meters long. It is now the New Mexico state dinosaur.

mountain ranges were formed. Then wind and water wore them away. New mountains rose. They too wore away. At times seas flooded the land.

About 225 million years ago, some of New Mexico was covered with shallow seas. The land above the water was swampy. Huge creatures called dinosaurs lived in the swamps. Some of them looked like giant reptiles. There were many, many dinosaurs. That is why this period is called the Age of Reptiles.

In time, the seas went down and the swamps dried up. The climate changed. And the dinosaurs began to die. Finally, they

dinosaurs
reptiles
climate

The *Dimetrodon*, also known as the "sail-backed reptile," once roamed parts of New Mexico. Remains of this dinosaur have been discovered near Jemez Springs. Some scientists say that the "sail" helped keep the reptile cool.

disappeared. The Age of Reptiles was over. Today, fossil bones of dinosaurs can be found in many parts of New Mexico. A fossil is a part of a plant or animal that has turned into stone. By studying the fossil bones, scientists learn about these strange animals.

Three museums in New Mexico show dinosaur fossils. Perhaps you can visit them sometime. They are the Ghost Ranch Museum at Abiquiu and the Natural History Museum at Carlsbad Caverns. The third is the Natural History Museum in Albuquerque. At these places students are able to learn many things about dinosaurs.

fossil

Shiprock in northwestern New Mexico. The Navajos have a legend that it was once a giant bird that brought their ancestors to New Mexico, then turned into stone. *Why do you think it is called Shiprock?*

The Mountains

For millions of years after the Age of Reptiles, the land continued to change. Volcanos sent clouds of smoke and ash into the sky. Hot lava spread across the land in many places and turned to black stone. You can see these black lava beds near Grants and Carrizozo.

Some of the volcanos formed high mountains. One of the largest is Mt. Taylor (3,471 meters or 11,389 feet). It is a holy place in the religion of the Navajo Indians. So is the famous Shiprock in northwestern New Mexico. This dark mountain of lava rock is shaped like an old-time sailing ship.

East of Raton is another famous volcano called Capulin Peak. It is a perfectly shaped cone. A road leads to the top. There, visitors can look into the crater.

The largest volcano in New Mexico was at Valle

Grande. This is in the Jemez Mountains west of Los Alamos. At one time, this great volcano was more than 4,200 meters (14,000 feet) high. The ash and lava that came out left a huge hole under the mountain. Then, about one million years ago, the mountain caved in. It fell into the hole. A valley 19.3 kilometers (12 miles) wide was formed where the volcano once stood. Today the valley floor is covered with rich grass. Cattle graze peacefully there.

Not all of New Mexico's mountains are old volcanos. In some places the heat and lava failed to break through to the surface. Instead, they pushed from below. Very

Capulin Mountain is an extinct volcano in northeastern New Mexico.
Can you find the rim of the crater?

9

The Land

Valle Grande in the Jemez Mountains of northern New Mexico is the crater of a once-active volcano. It is considered the largest extinct volcano in the world.

slowly, the land rose to form mountain ranges. The Sangre de Cristos near Santa Fe were formed in this way.

After all these changes, New Mexico finally became as we know it now. The highest point in the state is Wheeler Peak, close to Taos. It is 4,011 meters (13,160 feet) high. From the highlands in the north, New Mexico slopes gently toward the south. Still, there are some high mountains in the lower half of the state. At Ruidoso, for instance, Sierra Blanca Peak rises to 3,659 meters (12,003 feet). The lowest spot in the state is Red Bluff, near Carlsbad, at 877 meters (2,876 feet).

The Rocky Mountains come down into New Mexico from Colorado. In New Mexico, the Rockies are called the Sangre de Cristos. This name is Spanish. It means Blood of Christ.

There are other important mountain ranges in the state. The Sandias and Manzanos look down on Albuquerque. The beautiful Organ Mountains are by Las Cruces. The bright green San Juan Range lies in the northwest. The dry Guadalupe Mountains are in the south. And between Truth or Consequences and Silver City are several ranges in the Gila Wilderness.

Mountains are important parts of the environment. Because they are high, they catch rain and snow from the clouds. Tall trees grow on their sides. Thick grass grows in the meadows at their feet. Deer and elk graze in the meadows. All kinds of birds live in the trees and cliffs.

The federal government protects many of New Mexico's mountain ranges. These ranges are part of the National Forests. They are for everyone to use and enjoy. People go to the National Forests to hike, fish, hunt, and ski. In the fall they go to see the leaves of the aspen trees turn gold.

Plateaus and Plains

A plateau is a high tableland. It is mostly flat. But in some places, water has cut deep canyons into the table. At other places, hills and even mountains can be found on a plateau. Much of northwest New Mexico is covered by the Colorado Plateau. This plateau spreads over the area of the Four Corners. One of the most famous canyons here is Chaco Canyon. We will learn more about Chaco Canyon later.

About one-third of eastern New Mexico is plains. It is fine grassland. Herds of buffalo once grazed here. Cattle and sheep are raised on this land now. Along the Texas border is the Llano Estacado. This Spanish name means the Staked Plains. The Spanish explorer Coronado crossed these wide plains long ago. He said it was like crossing the ocean because the plains were so wide and flat. The waving grass seemed like waves.

Small plains surrounded by mountains are found in other parts of New Mexico. These are the dry beds of old lakes. The San Agustin plains west of Socorro are an example. The soil is rich and the grass grows tall there.

Many old lake beds lie in a *bolsón*. A *bolsón* is a closed valley. Water flows in, but it cannot get out. Water collects in shallow lakes. Later the sun dries up the water. The lake bed left behind is called a *playa*.

plateau
plains
bolsón
playa

A *playa* is very flat and often covered with salt.

In the Estancia Valley east of Albuquerque are many old salt beds. For centuries, Indians and Spaniards came and collected the salt. They used it on their food or traded it.

A young boy takes care of his grazing flock. From the back of his donkey, he can keep better watch. *What other kind of animal is in this picture?*

Rivers

The rivers of New Mexico are very important parts of the environment. They provide water for drinking and farming. They carry rich soil from the mountains to the fields below. Rivers provide a home for fish. Wild ducks and geese use their waters. Beavers, raccoons, and skunks live along the banks.

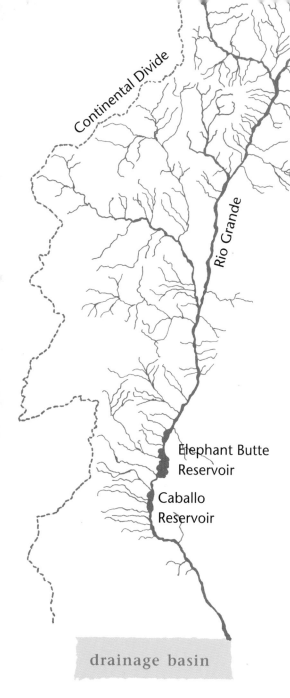

Continental Divide

Rio Grande

Elephant Butte
Reservoir

Caballo
Reservoir

drainage basin

People use rivers for fishing, swimming, and boating.

New Mexico's most important river is the Rio Grande. This river begins in the mountains of south-central Colorado. It enters New Mexico above Taos. The Rio Grande flows through the whole length of the state. It leaves New Mexico near El Paso, Texas, and Mexico. The river divides the state roughly into two halves.

The Rio Grande flows through steep canyons. But it also flows through narrow valleys where farming is possible. Farming is important in the Española Valley, the Albuquerque Valley, and the Mesilla Valley. Their fields are all watered by the Rio Grande.

More than half of New Mexico's people live in the drainage basin of the Rio Grande. A drainage basin is land drained by a river. Long ago, Pueblo Indians built their villages along the river. Later, the Spaniards came. They placed their towns near the river, too. Albuquerque, New Mexico's largest city, is on the Rio Grande. Las Cruces, the second largest city, is also on the river.

Without the waters of the Rio Grande, central New Mexico would look like a desert. Few people would live there.

Sometimes the river has too much water. Melting snow from the mountains or heavy rains can cause floods. The river overflows

into the valleys. Homes are destroyed. Fields are damaged. Dams have been built on the Rio Grande to keep floods from happening. The first was Elephant Butte Dam near Truth or Consequences. It was finished in 1916. Water caught behind the dam is used to irrigate crops in the Mesilla Valley. In 1925, the Middle Rio Grande Conservancy District was formed. Its job was to control floods. It did this by building more dams and better drainage systems.

New Mexico has other important rivers. One is the Pecos. It begins as a small, rushing stream in the Sangre de Cristo Mountains. It is joined by other streams to

The mighty Rio Grande flows down the center of New Mexico. For centuries, people have built their villages and towns along its banks. *Why is the Rio Grande so important to life in New Mexico?*

Elephant Butte Dam forms a large lake on the Rio Grande near Truth or Consequences. Elephant Butte can be seen in the center of the lake. *How do you think the butte was made?*

gypsum

form a true river as it leaves the mountains. The Pecos passes near Santa Rosa, Fort Sumner, Roswell, and Artesia. South of Carlsbad, it leaves New Mexico and enters Texas. Three other major rivers are the Canadian in the east and the San Juan and Gila in the west.

The Sands and the Caverns

Two features of New Mexico's geography are known around the world. One is the White Sands. The other is Carlsbad Caverns.

The White Sands are drifts of gleaming gypsum sand. They stretch for miles west

The great desert of the White Sands near Alamogordo. *What causes the ripples in the sand?*

of Alamogordo. Two rare animals live in the sands. One is a kind of lizard. The other is a small pocket mouse. Both animals are white like the gypsum. They can be found nowhere else. Part of the White Sands is a National Monument run by the federal government. Visitors are welcome. But much of the area outside the Monument is closed to the public. It is part of the White Sands Missile Range. Here rockets are tested.

Carlsbad Caverns is in southeastern New Mexico. It is one of the natural wonders of the world. The caverns, or caves, were first discovered and explored by a cowboy named Jim White, about 1901. The caverns

contain many miles of underground rooms. They are filled with beautiful rock formations. Millions of bats live in the caverns. Each summer evening they fly from the entrance in a large swarm. After feeding, they return before dawn.

Climate

Some people call New Mexico the Land of Sunshine. The state has only a few cloudy days every year. The dry, clear air helps persons with lung diseases. The air is pure and easy to breathe. For many years, sick people have come to New Mexico from all parts of the United States. Quite a few have been cured by the healthful climate.

But the climate is not perfect, of course. For one thing, there is not much rain. Some places in New Mexico receive only about 25 centimeters (10 inches) of rain a year. That is not enough to grow crops without **irrigation**. Irrigation means to bring water to the land from another place. Another problem is the spring winds. They dry out the earth and cause dust storms.

On the whole, New Mexico enjoys mild temperatures. Summer days around Las Cruces or Deming can be very hot. But at night the air cools and becomes pleasant. In winter, temperatures in the high mountains

irrigation

Early New Mexicans carrying water in a tank pulled by horses. *What might this water be used for?*

can drop far below zero. But few persons live in the mountains. So the cold is not a problem for most.

Vegetation and Wildlife

New Mexico has many different kinds of plants and animals. The kinds of plants change as you go from the desert and plains to the plateaus and mountains. That is because the **altitude** increases. As you climb in altitude, the temperature cools and rainfall increases.

Cactus, yucca, and mesquite trees are found at low altitudes. There the land is dry.

altitude

Irrigation Ditches (Acequias)

Irrigating means moving water to fields so that crops will grow. New Mexico does not have enough rain. So farmers must irrigate.

They dig ditches called *acequias*. These acequias carry water from streams and rivers to the farmer's thirsty field. From the ditches, water spreads over the land. It nourishes seeds of corn, wheat, beans, chile, squash, and onions.

Long ago the Spaniards and Pueblos dug the first ditches. They shared the work and also shared the water. The largest and deepest ditch was always called the *acequia madre*. That means the *mother ditch*. Little log bridges were built across the acequia madre where it crossed roads or paths.

Each year the farmers elected a ditch boss, known as the *mayordomo*. The boss was in charge of all the ditches in one area. His word was law and everyone obeyed him.

In the spring before planting, the mayordomo called the people together. It was time to clean and repair the acequias. He gave a job to each person. At day's end the mayordomo checked to see that the work was done.

Water in the rivers came from melting snow on the mountain peaks. Some years little snow fell. Thus the rivers were low. The farmers faced a water shortage.

The mayordomo told each farmer how much scarce water he could use. But some persons used more than their share and started fights with neighbors. Water was more valuable than gold, because without it there was no food for the table.

The mayordomo lets water into irrigation ditches by opening and closing ditch gates like this one.

Only plants that need little water can live on this dry land. Climbing to the plateaus and hills, you see different plants. Sagebrush and *piñon* trees grow there. These plants need a bit more water.

As you move higher into the mountains, great forests appear. The forests need much water. It comes from the heavy rain and snow that fall in the mountains. Thick groves of pine, spruce, and aspen grow here. On the tops of the tallest peaks, no trees grow. It is too cold and windy. Only hardy grass and a few tiny flowers can grow.

Each group of plants just described makes up a different **life zone**. A life zone is a part of the environment. It is different from the zone next to it. We know we are in a low altitude zone when we see desert plants. When we see groves of pine or spruce, we know we are in a high altitude zone.

Wild animals, like plants, live in different life zones. The deserts and plains are the home of antelope, coyotes, foxes, prairie dogs, and rattlesnakes. In the mountains live deer, elk, bear, bighorn sheep, bobcats, and chipmunks. Birds, too, have different life zones. The roadrunner and quail, for instance, like the lowlands. The bluebird, eagle, and wild turkey live in the wooded high country.

life zone

A modern-day buffalo herd grazes along the Santa Fe Trail in northeastern New Mexico. *What happened to the vast herds that once lived in New Mexico?*

The Balance of Nature

All things in nature must live together in balance. Plants, animals, and people all depend upon one another. That is called the **balance of nature**, or ecology. If the balance is upset, the environment can be harmed. It can even be destroyed.

People have often harmed the environment. They have disturbed the balance of nature. For example, a hundred years ago, people began cutting down New Mexico's forests for lumber. They did not plant any new trees. They let cattle and sheep overgraze the land. Grass helps hold the rain

balance of nature

when it falls. Grass helps keep the soil from washing away. But too many cattle and sheep ate the grass. The land was left bare. Wind blew much loose soil away. Hard rains washed out more soil. The wearing away of the land by wind and water is called **erosion**. When people cause erosion, they upset the balance of nature.

But erosion was not the only problem people caused. They hunted some birds and animals until they were all gone. In those days there were no hunting laws. People could hunt as much as they pleased. Along the Rio Grande, several kinds of water birds disappeared. On the plains, the buffalo were killed off. The same thing happened in the mountains with the grizzly bear, the elk, and the bighorn sheep. These animals disappeared from New Mexico.

Bighorn sheep.

erosion
conservation

Conservation

Conservation means protecting the environment. It means taking care of forests and grasslands. It means saving animals, birds, and fish. Conservation helps the environment.

The Bosque del Apache National Wildlife Refuge is home to many types of birds, especially during the winter.

wilderness
wildlife refuges

For many years, few people cared about conservation. Slowly, this began to change. New laws were passed. Conservation became important in New Mexico. About 9 million acres of wooded land were placed under the care of the U.S. Forest Service. There are five National Forests in the state. There are also several special areas of **wilderness**. Here, in the quiet of the forests, you can see New Mexico as it once was.

The first official wilderness in the United States was the Gila Wilderness, near Silver City. It was set aside in 1924 by Aldo Leopold. He was head of the Forest Service for New Mexico and Arizona. Leopold believed in conservation. He started the wilderness movement in the United States.

Seven **wildlife refuges** were also set aside in New Mexico. A refuge is a place of safety. Wildlife refuges provide a safe home for animals and birds. The Bosque del Apache on the central Rio Grande is one of the best known. The Bitter Lake Refuge east of Roswell is another.

The New Mexico Department of Game and Fish helps protect wildlife. It controls hunting and fishing and the sale of licenses. The department has also brought elk and bighorn sheep back to New Mexico's mountains. Animals brought from other states were set free in the forests. Now many herds of these animals once more live in our state.

Conservationist Aldo Leopold worked to preserve wilderness areas for the future.
Why should the wilderness be preserved?

It was my great joy to have shared Aldo Leopold's friendship. It was the true wilderness which attracted him—the places where he could go and be alone, the spots in the forests of New Mexico where a man could lose himself in his surroundings and be dropped back into complete comradeship with nature. We talked many times about the development of a wilderness area. There it would be possible to preserve scenic beauty and the wildlife.

—Senator Clinton P. Anderson, on his early friendship with Aldo Leopold.

These are important conservation steps. They show that some of the damage to the environment can be repaired. But we all must help. It is a big job. Even if we live in cities and towns, we can support conservation. We are part of the environment. We have a duty to protect it.

New Mexico's landscape has changed over the centuries. It is still changing. Part of the history of our state is the story of these changes.

Words to Know

altitude   culture   geography   plateau

balance of nature   dinosaur   gypsum   *playa*

bolsón   drainage basin   irrigation   reptile

border   environment   life zone   wilderness

climate   erosion   plain   wildlife refuge

conservation   fossil

Reviewing What You Have Read

1. Why is New Mexico called one of the Four Corners states?
2. What is the Continental Divide?
3. How do scientists know that dinosaurs once lived in New Mexico?
4. What town is close to the highest point in the state?
5. In what part of New Mexico is the Llano Estacado, or Staked Plains?
6. Name New Mexico's most important river.
7. Why was the Elephant Butte Dam built?
8. Why is part of White Sands closed to the public?
9. Tell why no trees can grow near the top of our highest mountains.
10. What is the balance of nature?
11. How does overgrazing cause erosion?
12. What are wildlife refuges?

For Thought and Discussion

1. How is the environment harmed when the balance of nature is upset? Give an example of how the balance of nature was upset in the past. Tell what happened.

2. Suppose that all of our state were flat and at the same altitude. How would the life zones be different? Give examples.

3. Why do you think parts of our state have been set aside as wilderness areas? Do you think it is important to have wilderness areas? Why or why not?

Archaeologists at work in one of the large
Indian ruins in Chaco Canyon, 1921.
Why do archaeologists study ancient ruins?

2

THE FIRST AMERICANS

The Indians have given much to New Mexico. They have lived here for many centuries. Long ago, their life was very different from life today. They had different ways of doing things and some different customs. But the Indians were also much like people today. They had families. They worked and played. They knew joy and they knew sorrow. As New Mexicans, we share the Indians' history.

Columbus made a mistake! When he landed in the New World in 1492 he thought he was in the East Indies. He called the people he found "Indians." We still use the word Indians. Today, they are also called

Native Americans. They were the first Americans. They really discovered the New World.

The story of the Indians reaches far back in time. Through archaeology we learn about their beginnings. Archaeology is the study of ancient people. **Archaeologists** are scientists. They dig in the earth to find **artifacts** of the earliest Indians. Arrowheads, stone knives, and pottery are examples of artifacts. By studying these artifacts, archaeologists can tell how the people lived.

The Hunters

The first Indians may have come from Asia long ago. Most people believe they walked across a land bridge to Alaska. Later, the land bridge disappeared below the ocean.

Once in Alaska, the Indians moved slowly south. They hunted animals as they went. Getting enough to eat was difficult. Life was hard and dangerous. These early Indians had to keep moving, looking for animals to hunt. After many centuries, the Indians had spread over all of North and South America.

For a while, archaeologists thought the Indians came late to America. They believed the Indians arrived only a short time before the birth of Christ. Then, in the 1920s, new discoveries changed all that.

archaeologist
artifact

With the bow and arrow the Indian could kill larger animals, even the buffalo of the great plains. *Where in New Mexico today might you see a buffalo?*

The first important discovery was near Folsom, New Mexico, east of Raton. A black cowboy named George McJunkin was riding his horse there one day. In an **arroyo**, or dry stream bed, he saw some giant bones. They were very old. McJunkin was curious. He took some of the bones back to the ranch. He told other people about them.

Later, in 1925, archaeologists came to the ranch. They went to the arroyo and found more bones. They said the bones belonged to a kind of buffalo that lived 10,000 years ago.

Stuck between the rib bones, the archaeologists found stone dart points. That proved ancient Indians had killed the buffalo. It also proved that the Indians were in New Mexico far earlier than people had thought.

arroyo

An early New Mexican family building a pit house.

The archaeologists called the stone points
"Folsom points." They were beautifully
made. To make the point, Indians had
chipped the stone carefully. Each Folsom
point was a work of art. Later, other ancient
points were found at Sandia Cave near
Albuquerque and on the plains near Clovis.

The Gatherers

About 6,000 years ago, the Indian hunters who made the Folsom points disappeared. Another group of people came here. The new people are sometimes called the Gatherers. They lived in the deserts of western New Mexico. They gathered *piñon* nuts, wild seeds, roots, berries, and herbs for food.

Finally, the Gatherers learned how to plant and grow crops. They planted corn. They also grew squash, pumpkins, gourds, beans, and cotton. Now their lives were better. With crops, the Indians had more food.

Folsom Point.

Mogollon and Anasazi

Farming changed the culture of the Gatherers. Some of them became the people we call the Mogollon. The center of their country was along the present Arizona–New Mexico border. The Mogollon Indians lived in pit houses, partly underground. They also built special lodges for religious services. Mogollon potters made fine jars and bowls of clay.

Farther north, other Gatherers developed a different culture. They became the Anasazi. They lived around the Four Corners. Anasazi is a Navajo word. It means the "Ancient Ones."

The Anasazi were **ancestors** of the

ancestors

The National Park Service has restored some of the ruined Indian homes in the Bandelier National Monument near Los Alamos. *Why is the preservation of ancient Indian dwellings important?*

cliff dwellings
pueblos

Pueblo Indians. They also learned to farm and make pottery.

At first, the Anasazi lived in pit houses like those of the Mogollon. Later, the Anasazi built **cliff dwellings**, like those at Mesa Verde, Colorado. They also put up four- and five-story apartment buildings in the bottoms of canyons.

Centuries later, the Spaniards called these mud and rock apartments *pueblos. Pueblo* is the Spanish word for town. Several hundred Indians could live in one apartment building. So each was truly a town. Today, Taos Pueblo still uses these old-style apartment buildings. Visiting there, you can get an idea how the Anasazi built their first towns.

We have lived upon this land from days beyond history's records, far past any living memory, deep into the time of legend. The story of my people and the story of this place are one single story. No man can think of us without thinking of this place. We are always joined together.

—Words of a Taos Pueblo man

Young girls take a walk across the bridge at Taos Pueblo.

Drawing of a Pueblo man and woman in ceremonial dress.

Chaco Canyon is south of Farmington. Almost a thousand years ago, it was a center of Anasazi culture. Chaco was an important religious and trade center. There were six or more large *pueblos* in the canyon. The largest was Pueblo Bonito. About 1,200 people lived there. The ruins of Pueblo Bonito now are a marvel to see.

The golden age of the Anasazi lasted for several centuries. Then things began to go wrong. There was a terrible **drought** between the years 1276 and 1299. Little rain fell. Crops failed and people went hungry. There may have been sickness and war, too. It was a bad time.

The Indians in Chaco Canyon and Mesa Verde left their homes. They and their neighbors looked for a better place to live. Some settled on **mesas** in northern Arizona. These were the people we later called Hopi. Others built new *pueblos* at Zuni and Acoma. But most of the Anasazi from the Four Corners traveled to the Rio Grande Valley. There the Spaniards found them in the year 1540.

drought
mesa

Pueblo Ways

The Pueblo people were not a single tribe. Each town ruled itself. There were even different languages among the Pueblos. The Zuni spoke one language, the Hopi another, the Jemez and Pecos still another, and so on.

There were many differences among the Pueblo peoples. But they also had much in common. All lived in apartment buildings of several stories. All were farmers. All made fine clay bowls and water jars. Most of them wove blankets. All had rain-making **ceremonies** as an important part of their religion. So, we can say all the Pueblo people shared a similar culture.

Sometimes the Pueblo towns fought one another. But more often they were at peace. Then the people could trade with their neighbors. They could visit friends and watch their ceremonial dances.

This man from the Santa Ana Pueblo knows songs that were old when the first Spaniards came to New Mexico.

ceremonies

A group of Pueblo Indians in front of their home in the 1890s.

The Pueblo Family

Several dozen families lived in each large *pueblo.* A family lived in one main room. The family members slept and ate in this room. They also did their family jobs there. Behind the main room were smaller rooms. Food was stored in these rooms. Weapons, tools, and extra clothes were also kept there.

The people used wooden ladders to climb to the upper stories of their apartments. If an enemy came, they pulled up their ladders. Then no one could enter. If the town was attacked, everyone ran to the rooftops. The men shot arrows at the enemy. The women and children threw down stones. Everyone helped defend the *pueblo*. Each town was a true fort.

Pueblo families always had several dogs. The dogs made good pets for the children. Believe it or not, the dogs learned to climb ladders! The Spaniards were amazed to see this. They saw the Indian dogs run up and down the ladders.

Each member of the family had jobs to do. The men planted and cared for the crops. In summer, they got up early. They went to the fields outside the *pueblo*. They spent the day hoeing and watering the plants. At harvest time, they brought the crops home.

Pueblo men also went on hunting trips. They went to the mountains to hunt deer and bighorn sheep. They went far away to the plains to hunt buffalo.

Sometimes women and children helped the men hunt small animals. For instance, everyone helped with a "rabbit drive." In a rabbit drive, the people made a large circle outside the town. Then they began walking toward the center. They shouted and made noise with sticks. Rabbits caught in the circle began running about trying to escape. The men threw curved hunting sticks and killed the rabbits. After the drive, there was plenty of meat for the *pueblo*.

Like the men, the women had their special

Pueblo Indian women grinding corn.
Which stone is the **mano**? *the* **metate**?

jobs. They gathered wild foods that grew along the Rio Grande or on the mesas. They fixed the family meals. They gathered clay and made pottery. They also built the apartment houses. Often the men helped with some of the heavy work. They would carry the large roof beams, for example. But the women made the walls and put on the mud plaster.

Children had their jobs, too. Boys helped their fathers in the fields. They scared away crows and other birds that attacked the crops. The boys learned to hunt at an early age. They practiced with bows and arrows and held contests to improve their aim.

Girls worked closely with their mothers. They learned to prepare food. They learned to grind corn with a *mano* and a *metate*. *A metate* is a bowl-shaped stone. A *mano* is a flat stone. The women and girls put corn in the *metate* and rubbed it with the *mano*. In this way they made cornmeal. From cornmeal, they prepared several different foods.

Girls also helped take care of the smaller children. They played with them while their mothers worked. They played games and made dolls of clay or corncobs. Pueblo girls, like the boys, learned to do their part for the family.

Food and Clothes

The early Pueblo Indians had no stores or supermarkets. They had to raise their own grain and vegetables. The Indians had no cows, sheep, or chickens. They did have turkeys. When they needed meat, they went hunting. But sometimes they could find no animals to kill. Other times no rain fell and the harvest was bad. Then the Pueblo people went hungry.

Corn was the main food. It could be prepared many ways. The Indians cooked cornmeal on a hot stone to make wafer bread. This bread was very thin, like paper. Today we use the Hopi word for wafer bread. We

This young Pueblo girl is dressed in traditional costume.

mano
metate

We came to the settlements called the pueblos *of New Mexico. We estimated they contained more than twelve thousand people, including men, women, and children. The people of each town came out to meet us. They took us to their* pueblos *and gave us turkeys, corn, beans, and tortillas, with other kinds of bread. They grind raw corn on very large stones. Five or six women work together in a single mill, and from the flour they make many kinds of bread. Their houses are two, three, or four stories high.*

—Explorer Antonio de Espejo, 1582

piki
posole
tewas
mantas

call it *piki*. Some corn was cooked by steaming it in an oven. White corn was boiled until it popped. This made a stew called *posole*.

Beans were an important part of each meal. Dried squash and pumpkins were also eaten. In summer, the big yellow squash blossoms were cooked and eaten. Wild greens could be gathered, too. After a hunt, there was fresh meat. This food was nourishing. It contained all the vitamins the Pueblo people needed.

Clothes were made at home. Each family dressed itself. The men wove cotton cloth on large looms. With this cloth, the women made shirts for their husbands. They sewed dresses for themselves and their daughters. Shoes called *tewas* were made of leather. These were brown and had high tops. Some Pueblos still wear *tewas* today.

The men also wove *mantas*, or cotton

Paintings by the early Pueblo Indians on the walls of a *kiva* at Coronado State Monument near Bernalillo. *What might these scenes represent?*

blankets. A manta was worn over the shoulders in winter. It was used like a coat. Blankets were also made of rabbit fur. They were warmer than mantas. It took many rabbit skins to make one fur blanket.

Pueblo Religion

The Pueblo Indians developed a rich and beautiful religion. They saw the world as a sacred place where everything fit neatly together. Stories told of a time when all people lived under the earth. Later, people left the underworld and moved into the light on the surface. When someone dies, the Pueblos believe the person returns again to the underworld.

The *kiva is* the center of religious life. It is a room that is partly underground. The only door is in the roof. People must enter by a

kiva

Dancers from Laguna Pueblo at the Gallup Intertribal Ceremonial held each August.

ladder. The most sacred ceremonies take place in the *kiva*. It is the church of the Pueblo Indians. Only members of the town are allowed inside.

The Pueblos have many kinds of ceremonies and sacred dances. Religious leaders are known as *caciques*. The *caciques* are in charge of the ceremonies. Some of the dances, like the famous corn dances, help bring rain and make the crops grow. The corn dances are usually performed in summer. Other ceremonies are used to cure sick people. Dances like the deer or buffalo dance give aid to the hunters

Through religion, the Pueblo Indians try to protect the balance of nature. They use their ceremonies to keep harmony in the world. During ceremonies, dancers must keep a "good heart." That means they must not feel fear, anger, or sadness. They must not worry. The dancer with a "good heart" feels kindly toward all people.

caciques

Indian Treasure

Long ago the Spaniards marched up the Rio Grande. They stopped at Cochiti Pueblo north of Albuquerque. On the edge of the village, they built a mission. A padre was left in charge.

Now, the religious leader, or *cacique,* at Cochiti owned a large gold nugget. The nugget was bright and sparkled, so he used it in secret ceremonies honoring the sun. In fact, he called all gold "seed of the sun."

The Cochitis were careful not to let the Spaniards know about the cacique's nugget. It was feared they would take it and the sun ceremonies could no longer be held.

In 1680 the Pueblos rebelled. They drove the Spanish colonists and padres south to El Paso. For a short time they remained free.

Then in 1692 the Spaniards led by Don Diego de Vargas returned. But the Cochitis were not ready to give up. Instead, they left their village by the river and fled to the top of a mesa. They took with them all their turquoise jewelry and the sacred gold nugget. This was the "treasure of Cochiti."

Once on the mesa, the Indian leaders decided that the treasure should be hidden. That was the only way to keep it safe.

At night the cacique and his helper carried the treasure down a steep trail to the bottom of the mesa. Under the waters of a rushing stream, they buried it. No one else knew where.

Next day the soldiers came. They fought a bloody battle with the Cochitis. Among those killed were the cacique and his helper. Now the location of the treasure was lost. The Cochitis searched for years. But they could never find it.

They returned to the river village. To this day they hold their old ceremonies. But without their "seed of the sun."

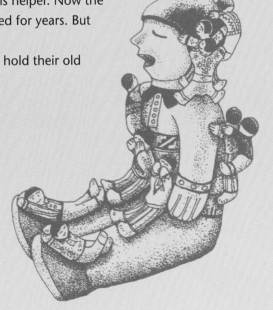

Storyteller figures like this one are the modern "treasure of Cochiti."

Apaches and Navajos

The Pueblos were not the only Indians in New Mexico when the Spaniards arrived. The Apaches and Navajos were also here. They had recently entered New Mexico from the north. Long before, they had lived in Canada. Both tribes spoke the same language, Athabascan.

The Apaches became scattered across New Mexico. Groups took different names. They even developed different customs. The Gila Apaches lived in the southwest, along the Gila River. They made houses called *wickiups*. The *wickiup* had a frame of willow poles stuck in the ground. The frame was covered with hides, blankets, or grass, and looked much like a tent.

The Mescalero Apaches and the Jicarilla Apaches settled on New Mexico's eastern plains. They lived in *tepees*. These were pointed tents that could be moved easily. The Apaches did not live in towns like the Pueblo people. They were always on the go. They traveled from place to place. They hunted deer and buffalo. They traded with the Pueblos. But sometimes they made war against them, too.

The Navajos lived in northwestern New Mexico. They settled on the land where the Anasazi had once lived long before. The Navajos built *hogans* for their families.

A tepee of the Plains Indians.
What are the advantages of tepees?

wickiups
tepees
hogans

A hogan, the traditional home of the Navajos. *What are the differences between the hogan and tepee?*

An old-style Apache wickiup, covered with bear grass.

Comanche men in the 1870s–1880s.

A *hogan* is a one-room house made of logs, stones, and earth. After the Spaniards came, the Navajos got sheep from them. With wool from the sheep, the Navajos began to weave their famous blankets. The Navajos were a hardy people. They grew in numbers in the harsh land of western New Mexico. Their tribe succeeded where others might have failed.

Utes and Comanches

The Utes and Comanches were two mountain tribes that lived in the Rockies. They both spoke the Shoshonean language. Between 1680 and 1700, they moved south into New Mexico. The Utes stayed in the high country above Taos. They remained mountain people. But the Comanches left the mountains. They took up new homes on the plains.

The Apaches claimed the plains, however. They

claimed to own the huge buffalo herds. The Comanches and Apaches went to war for ownership of the plains. The Apaches lost and fled west and south into the mountains. The Comanches were the new rulers of the plains.

Other Tribes

After 1750, several other tribes entered eastern New Mexico. They were the Cheyennes, Arapahoes, and Kiowas. They made friends with the Comanches. They helped the Comanches in wars against the Apaches and the whites. All these tribes are called Plains Indians. They spoke different languages. But the culture of each tribe was similar.

A Comanche woman in the 1870s–1880s.

The Plains Way of Life

The Plains Indians did not stay in one place and farm like the Pueblos. Instead, they followed the wandering buffalo herds. They loved the free life. They loved to travel on the broad plains.

The Comanches and other Plains tribes depended on the buffalo. The buffalo provided food, clothes, shelter, tools, and even musical instruments. Buffalo meat, fresh or dried, was eaten at every meal. Hides were made into moccasins. Soft hides

Early Tribal Locations

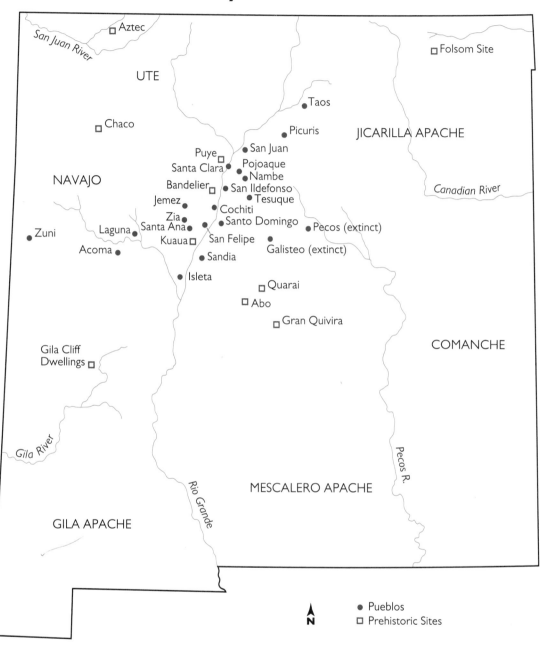

San Juan River

□ Aztec

□ Folsom Site

UTE

Taos

□ Chaco

JICARILLA APACHE

Picuris

Puye □

San Juan

Santa Clara

Pojoaque

Nambe

Canadian River

NAVAJO

Bandelier □

San Ildefonso

Jemez

Tesuque

Cochiti

Zia

Santo Domingo

Zuni

Laguna

Santa Ana

Pecos (extinct)

Kuaua □

San Felipe

Acoma

Galisteo (extinct)

Sandia

Isleta

Quarai □

□ Abo

COMANCHE

□ Gran Quivira

Gila Cliff
Dwellings □

Gila River

Pecos R.

MESCALERO APACHE

Rio Grande

GILA APACHE

● Pueblos
□ Prehistoric Sites

were also used for robes in winter. They were sewn together to make tepees, too.

Buffalo hair was woven into rope. The bones were made into tools. For a drum, the Indians stretched buffalo hide over a hollow piece of log. They put small rocks inside a hollow horn to make a rattle. No part of the buffalo was thrown away. Everything was used.

From the Spaniards, the Indians got horses. Riding on horses, they could travel far. They could hunt buffalo better. The horse became the most valuable thing the Plains people owned. Wars broke out as tribes raided one another for horses.

The Plains Indians spoke many different languages. As they moved about more, they had trouble understanding one another. So, they developed a new language that everyone understood. It was sign language. It was easy to learn. Simple signs were made with the hands. When many tribes camped together, the Indians all used **sign language**.

The Mansos

There is one more tribe that should be mentioned. It was a tribe called the Mansos. In Spanish, *manso* means timid or shy. The Spaniards called these people Mansos because they were meek and peaceful. They lived in the Mesilla Valley near Las Cruces.

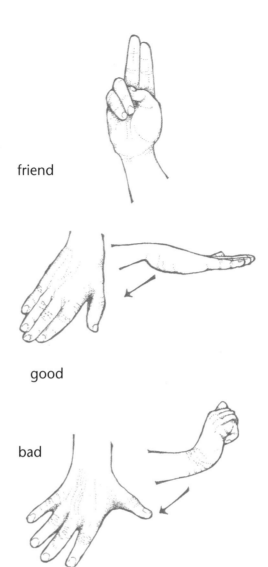

friend

good

bad

sign language

The Mansos were a small group. We do not know very much about them. After the Spaniards came, Mansos as a tribe began to disappear. No pure-blooded Mansos are left today. We do not even know what language they spoke. It is sad to think we know so little about the Mansos.

The Indian Contribution

The Indian people have contributed much to the development of New Mexico. As we follow our story, we will see the important part they have played. We will learn how the Pueblos, Apaches, and Navajos helped shape the past. We will also learn how they are contributing to New Mexico's present and future.

The Indians have much to teach us. Long ago, they learned about nature. They learned how to take care of the environment. They never wasted anything. The Indians treated the earth with respect. Now, their way of life has changed. They are citizens of the modern world. But they have not forgotten many of the lessons taught by their ancestors. The old knowledge they have saved from the past is still valuable.

Words to Know

ancestor	ceremony	*kiva*	*posole*
archaeologist	cliff dwellings	*mano* and *metate*	*pueblo*
arroyo	contribution	*manta*	sign language
artifact	drought	mesa	*tepee*
cacique	*hogan*	*piki*	*tewa*
wickiup			

Reviewing What You Have Read

1. From where did the first Indians in North America come?
2. Who were the Anasazi people?
3. Why did the Anasazi move away from Chaco Canyon?
4. Why do the Pueblo people perform corn dances?
5. What kinds of houses did the early Apaches have? Tell how these houses were built.
6. In what part of New Mexico did the Navajo people first settle?
7. Why did the early Apaches and Comanches go to war against each other?
8. Why were the buffalo so important to the Plains Indians ?
9. Why did the Plains Indians develop sign language?
10. Where in New Mexico did the Mansos live?

For Thought and Discussion

1. How did Folsom points help prove that Indians lived in New Mexico thousands of years ago?

2. Why did the early Indians have to learn how to farm before they could settle and build *pueblos*? Could Indians who did not farm stay in one place?

3. Why did horses become so important to the Plains Indians? If they had been farmers, would horses have been so important? Why or why not?

3

SPANISH EXPLORERS AND SETTLERS

To the Spaniards, America was a New World. They did not know what they would find here. In Mexico, they found gold and other treasures. The Spaniards hoped that they would find much gold in New Mexico, too. But they did not find any. New Mexico was a poor place. Poor or not, however, the Pueblo people loved it. They were ready to fight to keep their land. They did not want the Spaniards to take their land.

After Columbus's first trip to America, Spaniards settled in the Caribbean Islands. They built towns and cities. They farmed and mined for gold. And they looked north and west to the **mainland** of North

mainland

Hernando Cortés. *Why did Cortés conquer Mexico?*

conquer
capital

America. They hoped to conquer the mainland and find riches.

The Conquest of Mexico

In 1519 Hernando Cortés sailed west from Cuba with an army. He landed on the coast of Mexico. With his men, he marched through high mountains. At last they came to a wide valley.

In the center of this valley was a grand and beautiful city. It was the capital of the Aztec Indian Empire. The city had thousands of people. It was larger than any city in Spain. The Spaniards could hardly believe their eyes. How could there be such a beautiful city, unknown to them?

The Aztec Emperor was named Montezuma. He greeted Cortés as a friend. For a while, the Spaniards and Aztecs got along. But the Indians had much gold and other treasure. Finally, the Spaniards seized the gold. War broke out and Montezuma was killed. The great Aztec city was destroyed.

On the ruins of the Indian buildings,

Cortés began a new city. It became the Spanish capital. He named it Mexico City. In their own language, the Aztecs called themselves *Mexica*. Cortés changed that word to *Mexico* when he named the capital.

Mexico City became the center of government for a large Spanish colony. The colony was known as New Spain. It included all of modern Mexico and much of Central America. It also included a large part of what is now the western United States.

The Northern Mystery

Soon, other Spaniards left Mexico City to explore. They hoped to find another Mexico—a new Mexico. That is, they were looking for another Indian empire like the one conquered by Cortés. Perhaps, hidden in the wilderness, was a new Mexico rich with gold.

In the late 1520s Alvar Nuñez Cabeza de Vaca was shipwrecked on the Texas coast. With three others, he wandered lost for seven years. Two of these men were Spaniards. The other was a black slave named Estevanico.

After much suffering, the men reached the first settlements in New Spain. They had many stories to tell. They were the first Europeans to see new lands in the far north.

People in Mexico City listened to these

colony
empire

Exploration Routes of Coronado (1540–1542) and Oñate (1598)

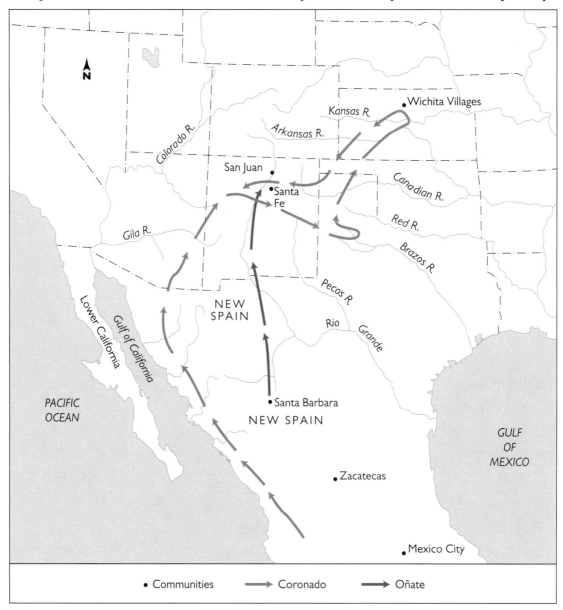

stories. They got excited. They thought Cabeza de Vaca had just missed finding treasure. Somewhere beyond the lands he visited must be the new Mexico.

Now, everyone believed that gold was in the far north. But where? That was the great mystery. For many years, the Spaniards tried to solve the "northern mystery." They tried to find the gold they believed was there.

The Journey of Fray Marcos

Fray Marcos de Niza, a priest, was one of the first to go north. In 1539, he went to explore. Estevanico, the black man who had been with Cabeza de Vaca, went along. He served as a guide. With Fray Marcos were some Indian servants.

The little party traveled up the Pacific coast of Mexico. They passed through the deserts of Arizona. Estevanico and several Indians went ahead. Fray Marcos stayed behind and waited for news. Marcos de Niza had sent Estevanico ahead to look for the rich cities he thought were near. Here is what Fray Marcos says happened next:

Estevanico and the Indians moved on. A few days later they came to an Indian town called Háwikuh. This was one of the *pueblos* of the Zunis. There Estevanico quarreled with the Zunis. They killed him. His servants

Estevanico left on the Sunday before Easter, after dinner. Some days later . . . Estevanico sent messengers back to me. They told me that I should follow after him, for he had found information of a very mighty province. One of the messengers said that Estevanico was in a town [that was] thirty days' journey from this province. The first city in the province was called Cíbola. He said also that there were seven great cities, all under one ruler. The houses of these cities are said to be made of lime and stone, and are very great. . . .

—Adapted from Hakluyt's *Collection of the Early Voyages, Travels, and Discoveries of the English Nation* (1810)

escaped. They ran back to Fray Marcos, who was coming up the trail.

When Fray Marcos learned of Estevanico's death, he was afraid. He did not wish to enter Háwikuh. But he wanted to see it. So he climbed a mesa. The *pueblo* was far away. But in the clear air, it looked to him like a great city. He thought it might be as large as the Aztec capital Cortés had conquered years before.

Fray Marcos hurried back to Mexico City. He said that he had seen a large city. He told what his servants had said about the seven cities of Cíbola. Now everyone was eager to go north. They were sure Háwikuh was filled with gold.

Coronado's Expedition

Francisco Vásquez de Coronado formed an **expedition**. Many Spaniards flocked to join him. On February 22, 1540, they were ready to start. As the expedition marched forth, there was much noise and color. Horns blew. Drums went rat-a-tat-tat. Men shouted. Horses and mules snorted. Flags waved in the breeze. Everyone was happy. The 300 soldiers were sure they would soon be rich.

The march north was long and hard. Water and food were not easy to get. Finally, Coronado reached Háwikuh. What a surprise! It was nothing like the great city Fray Marcos

This painting of Coronado and his men was made by Santa Fe artist Gerald Cassidy. *What did Coronado's expedition accomplish?*

expedition

Large Spanish stirrup like those used on the saddles of Juan de Oñate's men. *How does this stirrup differ from those you see today?*

thought he had seen. Háwikuh was a mud and rock *pueblo* of a few hundred people. There was no treasure, no gold!

Coronado still hoped to find riches beyond. He sent Pedro de Tovar to explore to the northwest. Tovar and some soldiers came to the Hopi pueblos. But they had no gold either. The soldiers moved on and some of them became the first Europeans to see the Grand Canyon of Arizona.

Now, Coronado's expedition moved east across New Mexico. It passed Acoma *pueblo,* high on a mesa top. The Spaniards arrived on the banks of the Rio Grande, near present-day Bernalillo. They found twelve *pueblos* in the area. The people spoke the Tiwa (or Tigua) language.

Coronado needed a place to stay for the coming winter. He chased the Indians from one of their *pueblos.* His own men moved in. Next, he attacked neighboring *pueblos* to get food for his men. The Indians fought back bravely. Many fled to the Sandia Mountains to escape the Spaniards.

In the spring of 1541, Coronado decided to explore the plains to the east. He heard a story that a great kingdom called Quivirá was there. The expedition stopped by Pecos Pueblo. This was one of the largest Indian towns in New Mexico. Then the Spaniards entered the plains.

For many weeks they rode east. Once a

hail storm hit. The large hailstones dented their steel helmets and frightened the horses. It was a difficult trip.

In the end there was no reward. Quivirá, in central Kansas, had no gold. It was a poor village of Wichita Indians. All the stories of treasure were false.

At Mexico City, the Spaniards decided that Coronado's expedition had failed. Coronado had found no great cities and no gold. The expedition had been all for nothing. The northern lands were just a wilderness. Only some poor Indians lived there.

The expedition, however, had not failed

Acoma Indian Pueblo, located on a mesa top, looks much like Coronado and Oñate might have seen it four centuries ago. *What were the advantages of building homes on top of a mesa?*

Quivirá

The explorer Coronado was the first to hear of Quivirá. With his men he stopped at Pecos Pueblo in 1541. The Indians there had an Indian slave brought from Kansas.

The Spaniards named this slave the Turk, because to them he looked like a man from Turkey. The Turk said his homeland was called Quivirá. It was filled with gold and silver.

The slave was smart. He knew these new men on horseback wanted treasure. When they heard of Quivirá's riches they would surely go there. And the Turk, guiding them, would get a free ride home.

So Coronado and his expedition left Pecos. They started for Quivirá. The Turk went in front, showing the way.

For weeks they rode over the grassy plains. They passed through the Texas Panhandle. The Spaniards crossed part of Oklahoma. Finally they arrived in central Kansas.

Quivirá at last! But where was the gold? And where was the silver that the Turk had told about.

The only thing to be seen was a village of the Wichita Indians. They lived in round houses covered with prairie grass. The Wichitas were as poor as could be!

The Turk had lied. There was no treasure in this land of Quivirá. He had fooled the Spaniards into bringing him home.

Coronado was very angry. He ordered the Turk killed. One of his men strangled the Turk with a piece of rope. That was the end of Coronado's treasure hunt. He then started for home.

A round grass house of the Wichita Indians.

In 1962, archaeologists uncovered the walls of Oñate's first Spanish settlement of San Gabriel, near Española. *What do these ruins tell about early Spanish life in New Mexico?*

completely. Much had been learned about the geography of the northern deserts and plains. More had been learned, too, about the Pueblo Indians and their neighbors.

Later Expeditions

For many years, no one was interested in returning to the far north. That land, now called New Mexico, was nothing like the old Mexico of the Aztecs found by Cortés. Forty years passed. Then interest in New Mexico began to stir again.

In 1581, three **missionaries** led by Fray Agustín Rodríguez entered New Mexico. But they were killed by the Indians. The Pueblo people remembered the harsh way that Coronado's soldiers had treated them.

missionaries

Drawing by José Cisneros of Spanish men as they might have looked about the year 1650. *Which of these men is wealthier? How can you tell?*

Signature of New Mexico's first Spanish governor, Don Juan de Oñate.

They wanted no more Spaniards in their homeland.

The Spaniards came anyway. Antonio de Espejo arrived in 1582 with a small party of soldiers. One of the men was Miguel Sánchez. He brought his wife Casilda and three small sons. Casilda Sánchez was the first Spanish woman to see New Mexico.

Espejo stayed only a short time. Seven years later, Castaño de Sosa brought another expedition. He hoped to start a settlement. That plan failed and Castaño de Sosa, like Espejo, left quickly.

Beginnings of the Kingdom of New Mexico

In 1598, a rich Spanish explorer entered the area. He was Juan de Oñate. Coronado had come to New Mexico looking for gold in the *pueblos*. Now, Oñate was looking for silver mines in the mountains.

But there is more to the story. Juan de Oñate brought settlers as well as soldiers with him. Spanish families in wagons were coming to live in New Mexico. There were men, women, and children. They brought sheep, cattle, and donkeys as well as tools for farming. These people were coming to stay. New Mexico would be their new home.

Here are part of the goods brought to New Mexico in 1598 by one of Oñate's soldiers:

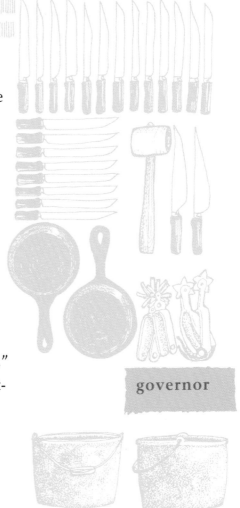

1 buckskin jacket	2 currycombs
2 saddles	1 iron file
16 horses and colts	2 kettles
16 oxen	2 frying pans
5 cows	2 swords
2 carts	4 pair of spurs
6 axes	25 butcher knives
2 hoes	400 needles (for trading to the Indians)
1 hammer for horseshoeing	

Oñate's long wagon train rolled north through present Chihuahua. It went up the El Paso Valley and the Mesilla Valley. It crossed the desert of central New Mexico. After months on the trail, it arrived in the Española Valley.

Oñate started a new town across the Rio Grande from San Juan *pueblo*. He called it San Gabriel. It became the capital of New Mexico. Juan de Oñate was the first **governor**.

Oñate set up a government. He called the country "the Kingdom of New Mexico." That was a grand title. It showed he expected to find silver mines. He hoped New Mexico would become a wealthy place. When it did not, New Mexico was later called a "province" instead of a kingdom. That was a lesser title.

governor

The historic Palace of the Governors at Santa Fe as it appeared in 1700. Its walls were begun in 1610.

Early Troubles

Some of the Pueblo Indians resisted the Spaniards. Several of Oñate's men were attacked when they went to Acoma. Oñate's nephew, Juan de Zaldívar and others were killed.

From San Gabriel, Governor Oñate sent an army to punish the Acomas. The soldiers attacked the *pueblo,* high on its mesa. There was a terrible battle. The Indians shot arrows and threw down stones. The Spaniards shouted their battle cry: *"Santiago! Santiago!"* They fired their guns.

The Indians were defeated. Arrows were no match for bullets. Many Indians died. Others were taken prisoner. Acoma was burned. It was a bitter lesson for the Indians. They never forgot their anger.

Back at San Gabriel, Oñate had other problems. No silver had been found. His settlers had grown unhappy. They thought New Mexico would be an easy place to live. Instead life was very hard. There were no comforts. So, some of the people returned to Mexico. They left New Mexico without asking the governor. That made things harder for the few settlers who stayed.

The Founding of Santa Fe

The king of Spain heard about New Mexico's problems. He decided to make some changes. That became easier when Juan de Oñate quit his job as governor. Don Pedro de Peralta took his place. He reached New Mexico late in 1609.

Peralta brought orders to move the capital away from San Gabriel. He looked around and found a place with water at the foot of the Sangre de Cristo Mountains. There, the new governor began building the town of Santa Fe.

During 1610, work continued. Peralta chose ground for a plaza. On the north side, the Governors Palace was built. Workers started a church on the east side. Families built their houses nearby. The full name of the new capital was *La Villa Real de Santa Fe* (The Royal Town of the Holy Faith).

Today, Santa Fe is the oldest capital city in the United States. The Governors Palace still stands. Now it is a museum. People still take

Statue of Gov. Pedro de Peralta on horseback. He consults with a surveyor in laying out the Santa Fe plaza in 1610.

Spanish padres and soldiers arrive at an Indian pueblo in early New Mexico. *What do you think the Indians thought when they saw these men for the first time?*

padres

missions

walks on the plaza. They also hold their fiestas there, just as the Spaniards once did. People from around the world visit and enjoy the capital city.

The Missionaries

The period after the founding of Santa Fe is called the Great Missionary Era. More than 30 *padres* built **missions** at the Indian *pueblos* around New Mexico.

One of the missionaries was Father Alonso de Benavides. In 1630, he wrote a report to the king. In the report, he told about life in the New Mexico missions.

Each *pueblo* had a mission church, said Father Benavides. There was also a house where the *padre* lived, called the *convento*. The *padres* taught the Indians many things besides religion. They taught them to read, write, and sing. They taught them to play music on horns and organs.

The *padres* also showed the Pueblo people how to farm like the Spaniards. They gave them new crops like wheat, onions, carrots, grapes, apples, and peaches. And they brought cows, sheep, horses, and donkeys to the Pueblos for the first time. But the Indians had to work at the missions. They had to follow the *padres'* orders. If they tried to leave, Spanish soldiers forced them to come back.

Growth of New Mexico

While the missions grew, new Spanish settlers continued to arrive. By 1630, there were 250 Spaniards in Santa Fe. Many others lived on farms and ranches.

In 1659, a mission was started in El Paso. At that time El Paso was in a part of New Mexico. Later, other missions were added. Some Spanish settlers lived near the missions. El Paso became an important stop on the road between Santa Fe and Chihuahua.

The Spanish population of New Mexico in 1680 was about 3,000. Santa Fe was still the only town. There were many more Pueblo Indians, perhaps 30,000. They were getting tired of Spanish rule. Soon there would be trouble.

Treatment of the Indians

It is usually said that the Spaniards were cruel to the Indians. Sometimes that was true. But the Spanish government tried to be fair. It tried to protect the Indians by passing laws. Often the laws failed.

Men like Coronado and Oñate treated the Pueblo people harshly. Some of the Spanish settlers did, too. Even the missionaries were mean and cruel at times. Some missionaries burned the Indian *kivas*. They tried to stop the dances and other Indian ceremonies.

At first the Pueblos were friendly toward the Spaniards. They were willing to learn new things. But they wanted to keep their own customs. They wanted to keep their own religion, too. But the Spaniards would not allow that.

The king and the missionaries did not want the Pueblos to have their own culture.

In a kiva at Santo Domingo, the Indian chiefs swore allegiance to the ways of the Spanish padres and Oñate. *But why do you think the Indians wanted to keep their own customs and ceremonies?*

The Spanish mission church at Acoma Pueblo, one of the oldest in New Mexico. The old convento is to the right. *Why would churches like this one sometimes serve as a fort during times of war?*

They wanted the Indians to give up their old ways. They wanted them to follow Spanish customs and think and act like Spaniards.

The Spaniards had one set of beliefs. The Pueblos had another. The Spaniards, for example, believed there was only one true religion, Christianity. The Indians believed all religions were valuable. Understanding was needed so that both peoples could live together peacefully in New Mexico. But in this case, understanding was not possible. In the end, there was a war.

On the morning of the following day, Wednesday, the Pueblos attacked Santa Fe. I saw the enemy come down from the mountains where they had slept. Mounting my horse, I went out with the few soldiers I had to meet them.

The enemy saw me and halted. They began to give war-whoops, as if daring me to attack them. Later they burned the church and many houses in the villa. We fought the whole afternoon. We passed this night like the rest, with much care and watchfulness.

—Governor Otermín's account of the Pueblo attack on Santa Fe, August 1680

The Great Pueblo Revolt

In early August, 1680, two Pueblo boys were given an important job. The boys were Catua and Omtua. They were asked to carry a message of war to other Indian villages. The message was in the form of a knotted cord.

Each Pueblo leader understood the meaning of the cord. Its secret message told them when they should attack the Spaniards.

Catua and Omtua were young and strong. They could run all day without tiring. They were proud to carry the cord from village to village.

But someone told the Spaniards what the boys were doing. The boys were arrested by soldiers. They were taken to Santa Fe. The Spanish governor, Antonio de Otermín, asked them questions. He wanted to know the Pueblo plans for war.

Catua and Omtua were brave. Neither one would tell the secret plans of the Pueblos. So, the Spaniards took them to a tree and hanged them. The boys died, but they were the first heroes of the **Pueblo Revolt**.

On August 10, 1680, the **revolt** began. It was led by Popay (also written Popé). He was a fearless Indian from San Juan Pueblo. He brought all the Pueblos together to fight the Spaniards.

On the Spanish ranches and farms, many people were killed. Others died along the roads trying to reach Santa Fe. Missionaries were shot or stabbed. Their churches were set on fire. The sky over northern New Mexico turned black with smoke.

The soldiers and settlers in Santa Fe went to the Governors Palace. Behind the thick walls, they prepared to defend themselves. Soon, hundreds of Pueblo warriors arrived. For ten days, the Spaniards and Indians fought. Many people were killed.

At last, Governor Otermín decided his people could fight no more. The Spaniards had to leave Santa Fe to save themselves. Hungry and afraid, the people marched out of the Governors Palace. They went south to

Pueblo Revolt
revolt

Acee Agoyo lives in San Juan Pueblo. He likes to run. He took part in a special race honoring the Tricentennial of the Pueblo Revolt.

El Paso. Later, they built new homes there.

Northern New Mexico was left to the Pueblos. The Spaniards were gone. The Indians were free once again. Most hoped that the Spaniards would never return.

The Pueblo Tricentennial

In 1980, New Mexico's Pueblo people remembered the Great Revolt. Now, 300 years had passed. It was a time to recall history. And it was a time to remember the Indian heroes.

During the summer of 1980, the Pueblos held special ceremonies and events. Boys and young men ran from village to village. They carried knotted cords. By running, they honored the memory of Catua and Omtua. Also, they honored their Pueblo culture. The boys of today were saying that they were proud of their people and their ways.

Words to Know

capital	empire	mainland	*padre*
colony	expedition	mission	Pueblo Revolt
conquer	governor	missionary	revolt
			tricentennial

Reviewing What You Have Read

1. Who was Hernando Cortés?
2. What kind of place did Fray Marcos think that Háwikuh was?
3. Why did the Spaniards think that Coronado's expedition had failed?
4. What did Juan de Oñate hope to find in New Mexico?
5. How was Oñate's expedition different from earlier Spanish expeditions?
6. What was the name of the town that Don Pedro de Peralta founded in 1610?
7. Why did the Spaniards not want the Pueblos to keep their own customs?
8. Who were Catua and Omtua?
9. Who was the leader of the Pueblo Revolt?
10. Where did the Spaniards move after the Pueblo Revolt?

For Thought and Discussion

1. Why did the first Spaniards in Mexico think that there might be rich lands in what is now New Mexico? Tell why they believed there was gold in the north.

2. Suppose that you were a Pueblo Indian during the Great Missionary Era. How would you feel about what the *padres* and other Spaniards were doing? Would you feel that they were helping or hurting your culture?

3. Suppose that you were a Spaniard during this same period. How would you treat the Pueblo Indians? Would you want them to accept your ways and beliefs? Why?

77

Spanish Explorers and Settlers

Governor Don Diego de Vargas.

4
THE SPANIARDS TRY AGAIN

History can show many things. It can show the terrible mistakes that people sometimes make. But it also shows that some people learn from their mistakes. After the Great Revolt, the Spaniards came back to New Mexico. This time, the Spaniards and the Pueblos became friends. More people came to settle on the land. New towns were started. It was also a time for new trade and travel.

Between 1598 and 1680, the Spaniards had worked to develop New Mexico. This was more than 80 years. But in the end, they failed. They ignored the rights and wishes of the Pueblos. So, the Great Revolt swept the land. It destroyed all that the Spaniards had built.

But the Spaniards were to get a second chance. They tried once more, after 1700. They started new towns and farms. The missionaries returned. Once again the yellow and red flag of Spain floated over New Mexico.

The Spaniards had learned a valuable lesson. Now they treated the Pueblo people with new respect. They tried to get along with their Indian neighbors. How all of this came about makes an interesting story.

The Reconquest

After the Great Revolt, the New Mexicans lived in the El Paso area for 12 years. All the while they were thinking of their old homes. They wanted to return to the upper Rio Grande Valley. They wanted to rebuild the New Mexico colony.

The chance came in 1692. Don Diego de Vargas decided to begin the reconquest. He was both a general and the new governor of New Mexico. Soon, he would become one of the most famous Spaniards in our history.

On August 21, 1692, Governor Vargas left El Paso. He marched north with Spanish soldiers. When he reached the northern Pueblos, he found that the leader, Popay,

reconquest

This statue of *La Conquistadora* was brought to New Mexico by the Spaniards in the 1620s. Today, it is carried through the streets of Santa Fe during special ceremonies. *What objects have you seen carried in processions or parades?*

had died. Some of the Indians were living in the ruins of Santa Fe. Many were ready to welcome the Spaniards back. With this good news, Vargas returned to El Paso. He told the people there to get ready. At last it was time to go home.

The next year, 1693, Vargas led a large expedition up the Rio Grande Valley. There were many families with their wagons. Cattle, sheep, and horses walked behind. There were soldiers and missionaries. Everyone was happy to be heading for Santa Fe.

Soon, however, Vargas and his people met

Albuquerque stands on the plains near the meadows of the Rio Grande. The villa itself consists of 24 houses near the mission. Some of the farmlands are good, some better. They are watered by the river through wide, deep irrigation ditches. Little log bridges cross the ditches.

The crops taken at harvest time are many and good. There are little orchards with grape vines and small apricot, peach, apple and pear trees. Delicious watermelons are grown. The citizens speak the local Spanish.

—What Father Domínguez saw at Albuquerque in 1776

trouble. Some of the Pueblos had decided to fight. Those living in Santa Fe did not want to give up their homes to the Spaniards. A fierce battle followed, which was won by Vargas and his men. Santa Fe was again under Spanish control.

The Spaniards brought a statue of the Virgin Mary with them. It was called *La Conquistadora* or The Conqueror. They honored the statue as a symbol of their religious faith. Afterward, they began a yearly *fiesta* in her honor. Each September, the tradition is continued with the Santa Fe Fiesta.

New Towns, New People

More time passed before the reconquest was complete. But by 1700 things had settled down. The Spaniards and Pueblos agreed to live side by side in peace.

In Santa Fe, damage caused by the Great Revolt was repaired. Settlers put up new houses. They rebuilt the burned-out churches. The old Governors Palace was cleaned and plastered with fresh mud.

Every year more people arrived from the south. Some of them settled in Santa Fe. Others farmed in the surrounding area. New Mexico was beginning to grow again.

Governor Vargas decided New Mexico needed another town. So, he led a band of settlers north and started a new town, near present-day Española. It was called the *villa* of Santa Cruz de la Cañada. Most people called it simply Santa Cruz. Now there were three *villas,* or important Spanish towns. Remember that the *villa* of El Paso was part of New Mexico then.

In 1706, a fourth town was added. In that year, settlers founded the *villa* of Albuquerque on the Rio Grande. Here, the land was good for crops. Tall cottonwood trees grew along the river.

Albuquerque was named for the Duke of Alburquerque. He was the **Viceroy** of New Spain in 1706. As the king's officer, he ruled over Spain's empire in North America. The *villa* of Albuquerque began as a small and humble place. But one day it would become the largest city in New Mexico.

Duke of Alburquerque. What is in a name? After the railroad came to the city in the 1880s, the first *r* was dropped. That is why the city name is spelled Albuquerque today.

villa
Viceroy

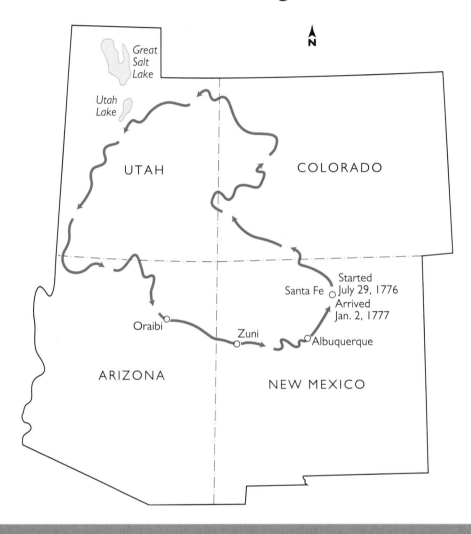

Explorers Reach Out

Over the years, Spaniards explored new lands surrounding New Mexico. In 1720, Captain Pedro de Villasur traveled north across the plains. He and his men reached Nebraska. There they were attacked by the Pawnee Indians. Villasur and most of his soldiers were killed. A few escaped and returned to Santa Fe. They told how the Spaniards had been defeated.

Another expedition set out in 1776. It was led by *padres,* not soldiers. Fathers Vélez de Escalante and Antanasio Domínguez were in charge. They were ordered to travel west. They were seeking a good trail to California.

The *padres* began their trip in late July. From Santa Fe, they headed up the Chama Valley. They crossed western Colorado and entered Utah. They traveled many weeks. Finally, they realized that snow and cold weather would soon make it impossible to go on. They had to give up and return to Santa Fe.

Escalante and Domínguez had learned much about lands west of New Mexico. But they failed to reach California. Many years would pass before the New Mexicans found a trail to the Pacific Coast.

Indian art showing warriors prepared for battle.

A New War

In those days of Spanish rule, New Mexico was like an island. In the center were the Spaniards and Pueblo Indians. Surrounding them in the great sea of desert and plains were other Indians. Indian tribes surrounded New Mexico on all sides.

In the northern mountains were the Utes. The Comanches lived on the eastern plains. The Apaches roamed across southern New Mexico. The Four Corners area was home to the Navajos. All these tribes fought the Spaniards. They also raided the Pueblos, who were now friends of the Spaniards.

The Comanche Conflict

The Comanches were the strongest enemies of the Spaniards. They had many warriors who were fine horsemen. Time after time they attacked New Mexico's towns and ranches. Hundreds of people died on both sides.

In 1775, a Comanche war party raided the Albuquerque Valley. As they were leaving, the warriors stole all the cattle and sheep from Sandia Pueblo. So, 33 Sandia men chased them on foot. The Comanches set a trap and the Sandias were caught. Every man was killed. It was a terrible loss for the *pueblo.*

The leader of the Comanche tribe was Cuerno Verde. That means Green Horn. He got his name from a hat he wore. The hat was made of buffalo fur. In the center was one curving buffalo horn. The horn was painted bright green. Cuerno Verde was the bravest warrior among all the Comanches.

Governor Anza

By the late 1770s, Spanish officials were worried. Indian raids against New Mexico were growing. It looked as if the Comanches might destroy all the province. What should they do?

In 1778, the king picked a new governor for New Mexico. His name was Juan Bautista de Anza. He was born and raised on the frontier of New Spain. Earlier, he had helped settle California. Anza was a good man to deal with the Comanches.

Governor Anza studied the problem after he arrived in Santa Fe. He decided to try to defeat the Comanches in battle. Then maybe peace would follow.

The governor put together a large army. There were soldiers and Spanish settlers. Many Pueblo Indians armed with bows and arrows also joined. This strong army rode north. Governor Anza led his men across the Rocky Mountains. They reached the plains of eastern Colorado. Then, as they had seen the Comanches do, the Spaniards set a trap.

Cuerno Verde and his band rode into

Juan Bautista de Anza.
What did Anza accomplish for New Mexico?

The Spaniards Try Again

the trap. Both sides fought long and hard. Bullets and arrows flew through the air. The brave Cuerno Verde would not give up. He was killed along with many other Comanches.

The New Mexicans had won a great victory. They shouted: *"Viva el Rey! Viva el Rey!"* (Long live the King!) Anza was very proud of his men. He took Cuerno Verde's hat with the green horn back to Santa Fe. Later, Anza sent the hat to the king as a gift.

The Treaty

Over the next several years, Anza held talks with the Comanches. At last, in 1786, they agreed to keep the peace. A meeting was set at Pecos Pueblo, east of Santa Fe. All the leaders of the different Comanche bands met with Governor Anza. The governor arrived wearing his best clothes. On his head was a hat with a large feather.

The Spaniards and Comanches agreed to a peace **treaty**. Instead of being enemies, they would work together. Anza gave the Indians a Spanish flag and medals with the picture of the king. One of the Indian leaders said: "Now the Comanches are Spaniards!"

About the same time, the New Mexicans made peace with the Navajos and Utes. Only the Apaches were still at war. But now

treaty

Colonial New Mexico

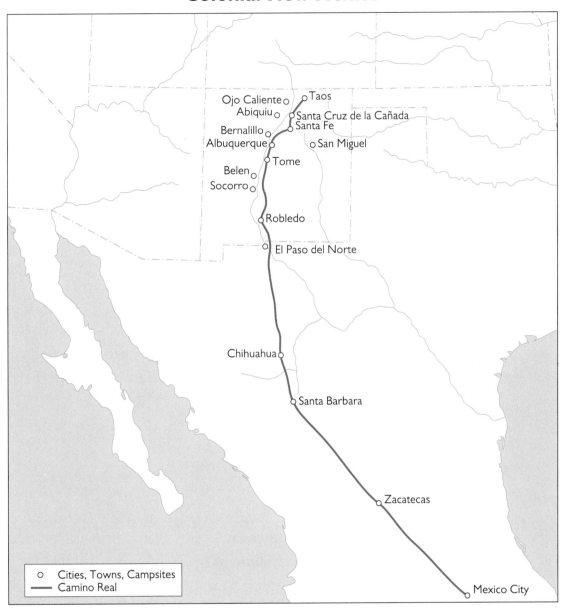

Taos
Ojo Caliente
Abiquiu
Santa Cruz de la Cañada
Santa Fe
Bernalillo
Albuquerque
San Miguel
Tome
Belen
Socorro
Robledo
El Paso del Norte
Chihuahua
Santa Barbara
Zacatecas
Mexico City

○ Cities, Towns, Campsites
—— Camino Real

Painting by José Cisneros of a Spanish soldier guarding a trader's caravan on El Camino Real.
What is he guarding against?

the Spanish settlers were safer than ever before. Governor Anza's treaties had saved New Mexico.

New Mexico Grows

Peace with the Comanches and other tribes allowed the settlers to expand. They could move farther away from the Rio Grande. Some of them took their families to the Chama Valley. They started towns like Ojo Caliente and Abiquiu. Others moved to the Pecos Valley. They dug ditches to irrigate their newly planted fields. New homes and towns were built.

By 1800, about 35,000 Spaniards and

Pueblos lived in New Mexico. It was the largest Spanish province in the far north. It began at Taos and continued south to Socorro. Between Socorro and El Paso, the land remained empty. That land was the hunting range of the Apaches. No Spaniards dared settle there.

This Spanish chest of cow or buffalo hide is the kind used by travelers on El Camino Real. *What can be said about the Spanish craftsman who made this chest?*

El Camino Real

Beginning in Mexico City, a road ran hundreds of miles northward. It went through Chihuahua City and El Paso. The road crossed the deserts of central New Mexico. It followed the Rio Grande to Albuquerque. It continued on to Santa Fe and ended in Taos.

El Camino Real, the Royal Road, became famous. Everyone entering or leaving New Mexico traveled on El Camino Real. For a time it was the longest road in North America.

caravans

The Caravans

Each year large **caravans**, or wagon trains, traveled along El Camino Real. From

The Spaniards Try Again

While his sons watch, this Spanish father yokes the oxen to a cart called a *carreta.* The drawing is by Betsy James.

What are the advantages of oxen over mules or horses?

Ox Carts of Old

For three hundred years the people of New Mexico traveled in ox carts. Teams of oxen were yoked together at their horns. The yokes were tied to the wooden tongue of the cart. After the cart was loaded, it was ready to go.

These old ox carts, or carretas, moved slowly. They went about 2 miles an hour. Thus it took all day to go only 15 miles.

Wheels of the cart were made of thick cottonwood. They were so heavy they squealed loudly when turning. Some drivers liked the sound and called it "the song of the carts."

But other drivers said the shrill noise hurt their ears. They would grease the wheels with buffalo fat. That helped keep down the noise.

Ox drivers walked next to their oxen instead of riding in the cart. They guided the animals with a long pole known as a *garrocha.*

This garrocha had a sharp iron point on the end. But the driver used it carefully. He did not want to hurt his oxen, just give them signals.

A light touch with the garrocha could turn an ox to the right or to the left. It could also signal him to stop. In this way the driver managed his ox team.

A cartwright was a carpenter who made ox carts. He knew how to pick out the best wood, how to shape it, and fit the pieces together. A cartwright was an important man long ago.

Today ox carts are gone from New Mexico's roads. A few can still be seen in museums.

Santa Fe and Albuquerque, they went on to Chihuahua City. The caravans were made up of wagons and ox carts. Men drove great flocks of sheep that were to be sold in Chihuahua.

The wagons and carts also carried other things to be sold. There were blankets, wool cloth, and socks, all made by New Mexicans. The leather shoes called *tewas* were also made for sale. Some wagons carried deer skins, buffalo hides, and dried meat. Others carried boxes of *piñon* nuts and bags of salt.

Families who wanted to go to Chihuahua brought their wagons and goods. They formed the caravan at a rendezvous on the Rio Grande. A rendezvous is a meeting place.

The governor in Santa Fe sent soldiers to the rendezvous. They were ordered to protect the caravan. Many men took their families with them on the trip to Chihuahua. Wives, young people, and children walked or rode in the carts.

The Apaches did not like the caravans passing through their country. Sometimes they attacked and the soldiers fought back. Most of the time the wagons got through safely.

Each night on the trail, the wagons formed a circle. The circle of wagons served as a fort. The people built a huge fire in the center. After eating, they sang and played

rendezvous

The Spaniards Try Again

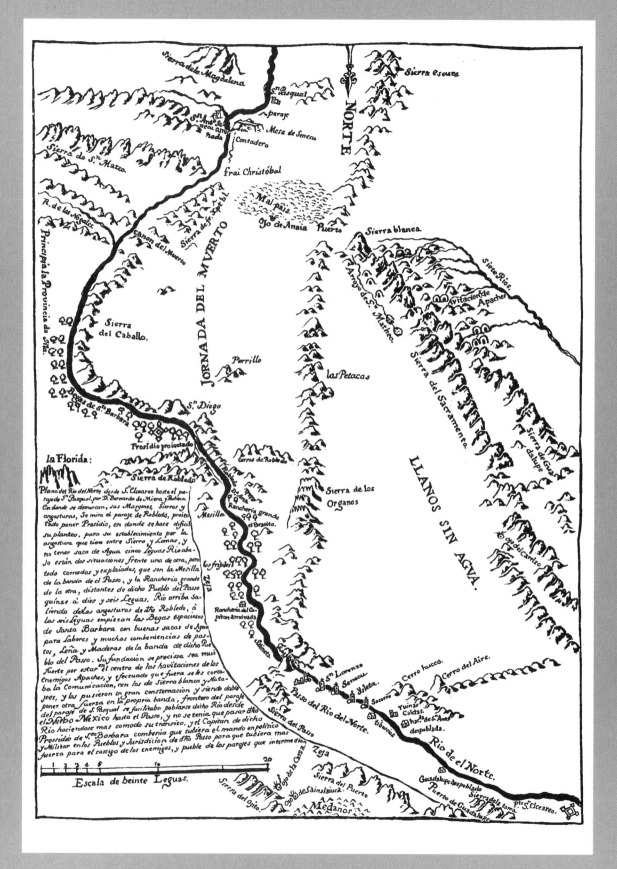

Sierra de la Magdalena

Sierra Escura

S.n Pasqual En

paraje

Mesa de Seneca

Contadero

NORTE

Sierra de S.n Mateo

Frai Christóbal

R. de los Nogales

Mal pais

Sierra blanca

Cañon del Muerto

Ojo de Anaia Puerto

Sierra Rios

Avitacionde Apaches

Arroyo de S.n Matheo

Sierra del Sacramento.

Principia la Provincia de Na.

Sierra del Caballo.

JORNADA DEL MUERTO

Perrillo

las Petacas

Sierra de Guadalupe

Vegas de S.ta Barbara

S.n Diego

Cerros de Robledo

LLANOS SIN AGUA.

Presidio proiectado

Sierra de Robledo

la Florida:

Mesilla

Sierra de los Organos

S.n de el Cantro

Rancheria grande

el Bracito.

Plano del Rio del Norte desde S. Eleareo hasta el pa-
rage de S. Pasqual, por D. Bernardo de Miera y Pacheco.
En donde se demarcan, sus Margenes, Sierras y
angosturas, Se mira el paraje de Robleda, proiectado poner Presidio, en donde se hace dificil
su planteo, para su establecimiento por la
angostura que tiene entre Sierra y Lomas, y
no tener saca de Agua cinco Leguas Rio aba-
jo están dos situaciones frente una de otra, para
todo comodas y explaiadas, que son la Mesilla
de la banda de el Passo, y la Rancheria grande
de la otra, distantes de dicho Pueblo del Passo
quinze à dies y seis Leguas. Rio arriba sa-
liendo delas angosturas de d.ho Robledo, à
las seis Leguas empiezan las Begas espaciosas
de Santa Barbara con buenas sacas de Agua
para Labores y muchas comberiencias de pas-
tos, Leña y Maderas de la banda de dicho Pueblo del Passo. Su fundacion se precissa sea mui
fuerte por estar El centro de las havitaciones de los
Enemigos Apaches, y efectuado que fuera se les corta-
ba la Comunicacion, con los de Sierra blanca y Na-ta-
jees, y las pusieron en gran consternacion y siendo dable
poner otra fuerza en la propria banda, frontero del paraje
del Nuebo Mexico se facilitaba poblarse dicho Rio desde
el paraje de S. Pasqual se facilitaba poblarse dicho Rio desde
Rio haciendose mas comodo su transito, y el Capitan de dicho
Pressidio de S.ta Barbara combenia que tubiera el mando en politico
y Militar en los Pueblos y Jurisdicion de d.ho Passo para que tubiera mas
fuerza para el castigo de los enemigos, y pueble de los parajes que intermedian

los frijoles

Rancheria del Ca-
pitan arruinada

S.n Lorenzo
Seneca

S.n Salineta

S.n Lorenzo

Ysleta.

Cerro hucca

Cerro del Aire

Paso del Rio del Norte.

Socorro

Tuinas
Caldas.

hac. de S.n Ant.
despoblada.

tiburcis

1 2 3 4 5   10   20

Escala de beinte Leguas.

Sierra del ojio.

Ojo de la Casa

Ojo de Sainalaiuca.

Zeja

Sierra del Puerto

Sierra del Passo

Rio de el Norte.

Guadalupe despoblado

Puerto de Guadalupe

Sierra dela toma

P.to S.n Eleareo

Medanos

guitars, and the young people danced. It was a time to have fun. It was a time to forget the dangers and hardships of the trail.

For many weeks the caravan rolled south. Wheels of wagons and carts sent up gray clouds of dust. The people grew tired. Still they traveled on. At last, the caravan arrived in Chihuahua City. The traders sold the goods brought from New Mexico. They bought other things to take home.

What were their shopping lists like? They included special foods like oranges, sugar, coffee, chocolate, and pepper. None of these things grew in New Mexico. They could buy fine cloth like silk from China and soft velvet from Spain. Wine, honey, and all sorts of medicine were available. Paper and writing pens, books, tools, nails, and iron locks might be on their lists. And, of course, they bought bullets for their guns.

When the buying and selling were finished, the caravan started back. A long trip lay ahead over El Camino Real. But everyone was glad to be going home.

This type of short sword was carried by Spanish soldiers on the New Mexico frontier.

This map of southern New Mexico in 1779 was drawn by Don Bernardo Miera y Pacheco, a Spanish map maker. *How does this map compare with a modern map of the state? What things are the same? What are some differences?*

95

The Spaniards Try Again

Zebulon Pike's Visit

Zebulon Pike was an officer in the United States Army. In 1806, he led a small expedition to the Southwest. The famous Pike's Peak in Colorado was named for him.

Pike and his men entered New Mexico while it still belonged to Spain. They were arrested as spies and taken to Santa Fe. The Spanish government did not allow Americans to visit New Mexico. They feared that Americans were looking for new lands to conquer.

Later, Zebulon Pike and his men were freed. When he returned to the United States, Pike wrote a book about his travels. In the book, he told about life in New Mexico. He told about what he had seen in Santa Fe and other places. From this book, Americans in the East learned for the first time about the far Southwest.

Pedro Pino Goes to Spain

cortes
elected
representative

Across the ocean in Spain, things were changing. In 1810, the people set up a *cortes*. The *cortes* was like the Congress in the United States. Representatives were elected to attend the *cortes* and speak for their people.

New Mexico was a colony of Spain. So, it was allowed to send one representative to

Engraving of Zebulon Pike.
Why did Pike go to New Mexico?

We came in sight of Santa Fe in the evening. It is situated along the banks of a small creek, which comes down from the mountains. The town has only three streets.

There are two churches with steeples. The houses have a miserable appearance. The public square [the plaza] is in the center of the town. On the north side is the palace, or government house. We dismounted and went in. The floors were covered with skins of buffalo, bear, or some other animal. We waited in a room for some time until the governor appeared.

—Pike's description of Santa Fe, 1807

the *cortes*. New Mexicans held an election—the first in their history. They elected Pedro Pino of Santa Fe. He would be their first representative in the *cortes*.

Friends took up money for Pedro Pino. The money helped pay his way to Spain. Pedro Pino went down El Camino Real to Chihuahua City. From there he rode to Mexico City. Then he went to the East Coast and got on a ship to Spain.

In Spain, Pino took his seat in the *cortes*. The other representatives had hardly heard of New Mexico. It was far away and they knew little about it. Pedro Pino made speeches. He told about New Mexico's problems. It was a poor colony and needed help from Spain.

Spain, however, had little money then. The members of the *cortes* said New Mexico would have to help itself. So Pedro Pino went home with nothing. The New Mexicans would have to solve their own problems.

End of the Colonial Period

colonial period

New Mexico became a Spanish colony in 1598. It remained part of Spain's empire for the next 200 years. This time is known as the **colonial period** in New Mexico history.

The colonial period came to an end in 1821. In that year, the people of New Spain decided to set up an independent nation. They called the new nation Mexico. No longer would the king of Spain rule their lives.

New Mexico became part of independent Mexico. The capital of the nation remained at Mexico City. The next 25 years in the history of New Mexico are called the "Mexican Period." It lasted from 1821 to 1846.

In the next chapter, we will take one more look at the colonial period. We will study the lives of the Spanish settlers. We will see how they lived, worked and dressed. We will try to discover what they thought and how they felt about things.

It is important that we understand them as real people. They lived centuries ago. But the men, women, and children were much like ourselves. We will get to know them better.

Words to Know

caravan   reconquest   treaty

colonial period   rendezvous   viceroy

cortes   representative   *villa*

elect

Reviewing What You Have Read

1. What lessons did the Spaniards learn from the Great Pueblo Revolt?
2. Who led the reconquest of New Mexico in 1692?
3. How did the Apaches, Utes, Navajos, and Comanches feel about the Spaniards returning to New Mexico?
4. Who was Cuerno Verde?
5. What did Governor Juan Bautista de Anza decide to do about the Comanches?
6. Why did no Spaniards settle between Socorro and El Paso?
7. What was El Camino Real?
8. Why did caravans travel from New Mexico to Chihuahua?
9. Why did the Spaniards arrest Zebulon Pike and his men?
10. For what reason did Pedro Pino go to Spain?
11. Why did the colonial period in New Mexico come to an end in 1821?

For Thought and Discussion

1. Why do you think that many Pueblos were not against the Spaniards returning to New Mexico in 1692? Why were many ready to welcome the Spaniards back?

2. During the days of Spanish rule, in what ways was New Mexico "like an island"?

3. How did Governor Anza's treaties help to save New Mexico? What might have happened if these treaties had not been made?

5

SPANISH COLONIAL LIFE

Ways of living change. Children do not live like their grandparents. They think new thoughts. They do new things. However, we should not forget the old ways. They are a part of our history. The old ways show us what our ancestors were like. They can help us understand what life was like long ago. We can compare our customs today with those of the past. Then we can see how we are like our ancestors. We can also see how we are different.

Did you ever want to be a **pioneer**? Do you think it would be fun to cross the plains in a covered wagon, or go hunting buffalo, or make your own clothes from animal skins?

pioneer

The pioneers helped make our nation. They helped begin our cities, towns, farms, and ranches. The United States was built on the hard work of the pioneers.

Daniel Boone of Kentucky was a well-known American pioneer. He wore a raccoon cap with the tail hanging down. He dressed in leather clothes. He carried a long rifle to protect his family. He used an ax to chop down tall trees. From the trees, he built a log cabin.

Daniel Boone's wife worked in the garden. Inside the cabin, she cooked and sewed. The children played on the floor in front of the fireplace. They helped their mother and father with family work. This was the life of an American pioneer family.

In New Mexico, the Spanish pioneers had a different way of doing things. Their customs were not like those of the Boone family. New Mexico was different from Kentucky. The land was different. The climate was different. Pioneers in New Mexico had a different kind of life.

The People

What kind of people were the Spaniards? How did they live their lives? What did they think about things? These questions are hard to answer, but we can try.

American pioneers in other parts of the country built homes like this log cabin.

In New Mexico, Spanish settlers built flat-roofed adobe homes. *Why might adobe be better suited to New Mexico than a log cabin?*

A family of Hispanic farmers in New Mexico
about a century ago.

First, we know that the Spaniards were
brave. Anyone who starts a new home on
the frontier has to be brave. The frontier is
the land on the edge of the wilderness.
All around are many dangers. Only strong
and brave people can make a home on the
frontier.

Second, the Spaniards helped their
neighbors. Pioneer families must work

Drawing by Betsy James of a Pueblo Indian selling baskets to a Spanish mother. *What other ways might neighbors have helped each other?*

together. Life is hard. So helping each other is a lesson that must be learned at once.

Third, the Spaniards, like all pioneers, knew how to do many jobs. They knew about farming and how to take care of farm animals. They could build houses and make their own clothes. They even gathered wild plants and made their own medicine. Living on the frontier, people must learn how to take care of themselves.

Finally, the Spaniards were a very proud people. They were proud of their religion and the Spanish king. They were proud of their Spanish culture.

A typical New Mexican farm house.
Note the chile drying.

In the month of September, 1875, 50 men from villages around Lucero decided to go buffalo hunting. Lucero in those days was a starting point for hunts. It was called the town of the Ciboleros. Thirty wagons were prepared. After a week of slow traveling, the hunters reached the great herds of buffalo on the plains. The men made camp and laid plans to begin the hunt the next day. Seventeen men killed the buffalos. The rest skinned the animals and prepared the meat so it would not spoil.

After six days of hunting, over 100 buffalos had been killed. Then the wagons started home. There was great joy in every family when the fathers returned with much buffalo meat.

—Samuel Montoya's account of the ciboleros

Their Food

Besides air and water, people need three things to live. Those things are food, clothes, and shelter. For the pioneers, food was most important. It was the first thing they had to get for their families.

On the frontier, men hunted for meat. In New Mexico, they hunted deer and elk in the mountains. During September, they hunted buffalo on the plains.

Buffalo hunters were called *ciboleros*. They dressed in leather shirts. On their heads, they wore leather hats with a feather. They carried spears to kill the buffalo. Each *cibolero* had a hunting horse. This horse could run fast. It carried the rider close to the buffalo so he could kill it with his spear.

ciboleros

Before Super Markets

The early Spaniards did not have stores. When they wanted to buy something, they went to an outdoor market. Markets were held on certain days of the week. On those days, the country people came to town to sell or trade farm products.

Often the Pueblo Indians came to the market. If you want to know what the old-time markets were like, visit the plazas at Santa Fe or Albuquerque. The Pueblo people still come there. Now they sell things to tourists, like jewelry and pottery. But sometimes they sell bread, fruit, chile, and *piñon* nuts. These were the same things sold long ago.

Once a year, many towns held a **trade fair**. This was just a large market that lasted a week or more. The people came to trade, but also to have fun. They played games of all kinds. There were horse races. Tasty food was cooked and sold to visitors.

The largest trade fair was at Taos. This fair was held in September. People from as far as Chihuahua came. The Comanches came from the plains with buffalo meat and hides to trade. The Utes rode down from the Rockies. Hundreds of people camped at Taos for the fair.

Sometimes the Spanish governor from Santa Fe attended the fair. He brought soldiers with him to keep order because the fairs were wild and noisy. Often there was trouble. But when the governor was there, most people tried to behave.

An old custom at New Mexico fairs was "the truce of God." That meant that all people could travel to a fair in safety. Under the truce, Indians would not bother the Spaniards. And Spanish soldiers did not attack Comanches, Apaches, or other tribes coming to trade. The "truce of God" helped keep the peace at fair time.

A scene from the Taos re-enactment of the old colonial trade fairs.

After the hunt, the *ciboleros* put the meat and hides into a wagon. They also took fresh bones. Their wives would make soup from the bones during the coming winter. The pioneer children loved buffalo bone soup.

Only a small part of the Spaniards' food came from hunting. Their own sheep and cows provided meat through the year. They also raised goats for milk. From the goat milk, they made a soft white cheese.

Other foods came from fields, gardens, and orchards. Wheat and corn were raised to make bread. The Spaniards grew vegetables in their gardens. They grew beans, peas, carrots, lettuce, onions, and garlic. Chile was another important crop. Red or green, it took the place of pepper. Also, chile has a lot of Vitamin C. This is one of the most important vitamins for keeping people healthy.

The Spaniards had many fruit trees. In the fall, the fruit was dried in the sun. During the winter, boys and girls ate dried fruit like candy.

Spanish mothers gathered wild plants for food. Along streams and in the mountains, they found wild raspberries and chokecherries. Some years there was a good crop of *piñon* nuts. Children roasted the nuts in the fireplace. Then they cracked them open with their teeth. Another food was wild spinach, called *quelites*.

A cibolero or buffalo hunter painted on wooden panel from a house at Santa Cruz de la Cañada.

trade fair

Their Clothes

Governor Juan de Oñate brought fine clothes to New Mexico in 1598. He and his men had fancy suits with lace collars. The women brought pretty dresses made of silk. But those were not the clothes a person wore every day on the frontier.

Very soon people learned that simple clothes were best for life in New Mexico. Most men dressed in leather suits like the *ciboleros*. Or they wore plain pants and shirts made of cotton cloth. Only a few very rich ranchers continued to buy clothes from Mexico or Spain.

The Spanish soldiers, of course, had uniforms. They wore blue jackets and pants with red cuffs. Their hats were black. They also had vests made of leather. The vests were so thick they protected the soldiers from Indian arrows.

Women dressed in blouses and skirts that came just below the knees. Each one had a *rebozo*. That was a shawl that wrapped around the face and neck. The *rebozo* protected the head from sun and wind. Women also had to cover their heads with a *rebozo* when they went inside a church.

The fancy dress of a New Mexican rancher of the 1800s.

rebozo

Their Houses

In the forests of Kentucky, pioneers put up log cabins. But in New Mexico, the Spanish settlers built houses of *adobe* brick. These bricks are easy to make. Clay, sand, water, and a little straw are mixed together. Next, this mix is put into a wooden mold. Then, the mold is removed. The sun dries the mud until it is hard, making a brick.

Making adobe bricks by hand is hard work.
Why is adobe the most common building material in New Mexico?

These bricks were stacked up, with mud in between, to form walls. Houses, churches, and even the Governors Palace were made in this way. On top of the walls, large logs were placed. The logs were called *vigas*. They held up the roof.

Adobe bricks make good houses. The walls are thick, so the rooms stay cool in the hot summer. In winter, small corner fireplaces kept the houses warm. Some larger buildings had an open patio in the center. In New Mexico, this area was called a *placita*. In nice weather, people used the open *placita* like another room.

Most houses had an outdoor adobe oven. This oven was half-round and very large.

adobe
vigas
placita

This *horno* sits next to an adobe house. *How does this oven compare with the oven at your home?*

horno
occupation

Many loaves of bread could be baked at one time. The oven was called an *horno*. *Hornos* can be seen today among the Pueblo Indians. The Pueblos learned how to make *hornos* from the Spaniards.

Occupations

An **occupation** is the job a person does for a living. A nurse, a baker, a farmer, and an engineer each has a different occupation. Some jobs of Spanish New Mexicans have not changed. In the old days, many people farmed the land. Others raised cattle and sheep. The occupations of farmer and rancher still exist today.

But many other jobs the Spaniards once held are gone. Times have changed. Those old jobs are no longer needed. People have new occupations that are needed in today's world.

In blacksmith shops like this one, Spanish workers made the iron and steel goods needed by the settlers.
What important items would these men have made?

Let's look at some of the old Spanish occupations. They will show us how the pioneers in New Mexico made a living.

The Blacksmith *(El Herrero)*

The blacksmith made things of iron. People liked to come to the blacksmith's shop. They watched him heat iron in a fire. When the iron was very hot, it became soft. The blacksmith then shaped it with his hammer. From the hot iron, he made shoes for horses. He also made all the other metal things used by the Spanish pioneers.

These mule packers are loading up for the trail.

Can you guess why the mule is blindfolded?

The Miller *(El Molinero)*

There was a mill on most streams in northern New Mexico. Each mill had a wheel with wooden blades. The water flowing in the stream hit the blades and turned the wheel. The wheel turned two large grinding stones. Each fall, after the harvest, wheat and corn were ground between these stones.

The miller did the grinding. He owned the mill. Farmers brought him grain. The miller put the grain between the turning stones. Out came flour, ready for making bread or *tortillas*. Often the farmers had no money to pay for the grinding, so they gave the miller part of the flour in return for grinding it.

The Mule Driver *(El Arriero)*

Mule drivers were like today's truck drivers. They carried goods over long distances. Only they used mules, not trucks, to carry things.

Long lines of mules crossed the mountain trails. They brought corn and wool from small villages to Santa Fe. Sometimes the drivers took their mules down El Camino Real. They traveled with the fall caravan to Chihuahua.

The Sheepherder
(El Pastor)

Ranchers on the Rio Grande hired men to herd their sheep. These sheepherders took the flocks to the mesas and mountains to graze. The men who did this work were very poor. For months they lived outdoors. They cooked on campfires. Their only helpers were smart dogs. The dogs ran around the flock and kept the sheep together.

Spanish weavers wove cloth on large looms like this one. *Where can you see people using looms today?*

The Weaver
(El Tejedor)

Weavers wove cloth on a large loom. They also wove blankets and rugs. In New Mexico, both men and women were weavers. Spanish women had few occupations. They had to take care of the house and children. But weaving was something they could do at home.

Weaving is one job from Spanish days that still exists. Weavers work today in Chimayó, Truchas, and other towns. The fine blankets they make are famous.

The Irrigation Ditches

Irrigation provided vital water to fields and farms.

Irrigation ditches, called *acequias,* were an important part of life in Spanish New Mexico. The ditches carried water through the towns and villages. Women went to the ditches with clay jars. They filled them with water and carried the jars home on their heads.

Spanish pioneers got water for drinking and bathing from the ditches. Horses and cows drank at the ditches, too. But most of the water went to irrigate the fields. Without this irrigation water, the crops would die.

Every spring, the ditches had to be cleaned out. Everyone worked together. Each family who lived along the ditch did its part. That was a pioneer custom. People living along ditches today still follow the old custom.

A Family Life

Spanish families were large. There were many children. Grandparents and other relatives might also live in the house. All shared in the work.

A new family began when a man and woman married. Parents made the plans for the wedding. The young man's father went to the bride's house. He asked her parents to give permission for the marriage. If they said yes, then a date for the wedding could be set.

The young man paid for the bride's wedding dress. He also gave her a large trunk. In the trunk were things such as clothes, shoes, and a ring.

A day or two before the wedding, the church was cleaned and decorated. Those attending put on their best clothes. After the wedding in the church, special food was served. There was music and dancing. It was a happy time for the whole town.

Musicians, followed by the bride and groom, lead a wedding procession. This custom dates back to Spanish colonial days. *How does this compare with wedding customs in your community today?*

The home-life of the New Mexican family interested me greatly. The large, roomy adobe house was not like my New England homestead. The beds were covered with Navajo blankets. The food, though new to me, was very good. Beef was stewed with hot but delightful chile.

In the evenings we gathered by the light of the adobe fireplace. We sang the sweet Spanish folk-songs or played happy, simple games. One game was called Florón (The Ring). It is very much the same as "Button, button, who's got the button?" except that a ring is passed from hand to hand instead of a button.

—Charles Lummis, on a visit to the house of Manuel Chaves

As children were born and grew up, they learned to help their mother and father. They carried firewood and water. They worked in the garden. They also helped take care of the farm animals. On the frontier, boys and girls had to work very hard.

But there was also a time for fun. Children had many games. A favorite was **shinny**. Shinny is like hockey. Players hit a ball on the ground with a stick. The team making the most points wins. Both Pueblo and Spanish children played shinny.

On winter nights, the family sat in front of the fireplace. Grandfathers told stories from Spain. Children sang songs. Everyone asked riddles. Riddles are puzzles. You must think very hard to solve them.

shinny

Here is one of the old Spanish riddles:

Chiquita como un ratón,
Y guarda la casa como
un león.
    (La llave)

What's small as a mouse
And guards the house like
a lion?
    (Answer: A Key)

Religious Life

The church was the center of village life in New Mexico. There were many religious holidays. Christmas and Easter were most important. But many saints' days were celebrated, too.

May 15, for example, was the day of San Ysidro. This saint helped farmers. On his day, the people carried a statue of San Ysidro into the fields. The priest blessed the crops. After that everyone hoped for a good harvest.

This drawing shows San Ysidro in the fields with oxen and a plow.

Land Grants

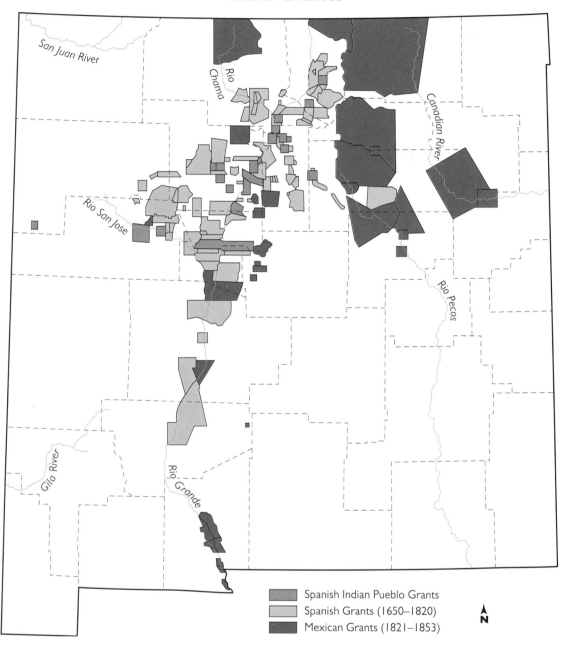

San Juan River

Rio Chama

Canadian River

Rio San Jose

Rio Pecos

Gila River

Rio Grande

Spanish Indian Pueblo Grants
Spanish Grants (1650–1820)
Mexican Grants (1821–1853)

N

Land Grants

All pioneers need land. They need land for new towns. They need land for farming and ranching. The Spanish government knew this. So the government worked out a plan to give land to the settlers.

The people who asked for land were given grants, known as *mercedes*. Each farm family got a piece of land as a grant. People in villages and towns got one large grant. They owned it all together. This was a good way for the Spanish pioneers to get the land they needed.

Much later, there were problems over these **land grants**. When the Americans came, they did not understand the Spanish way of giving land. Because of that, many New Mexicans lost their lands. Some of the land problems are still unsolved.

The Spanish Contribution

The culture of Spain has left its mark on New Mexico. Many houses and public buildings are built in the Spanish style. Many of our foods, laws, and customs are like those of Spain. Towns, rivers, and mountains often have Spanish names. Without Spain's pioneers, New Mexico would be a very different place today.

land grant

Words to Know

adobe	land grant	pioneer	*rebozo*	trade fair
cibolero	occupation	*placita*	shinny	*viga*
horno				

Reviewing What You Have Read

1. Who were the *ciboleros?*
2. Why was the chile important to the early Spaniards?
3. How are adobe bricks made?
4. What kinds of things did the pioneer blacksmiths make?
5. How did the Spanish farmers often pay the miller for grinding?
6. Why were dogs important to the Spanish sheepherders?
7. What was one occupation that some Spanish women had during colonial times?
8. Why were *acequias,* or irrigation ditches, important to the farmers?
9. Describe the game of shinny.
10. What were land grants?

For Thought and Discussion

1. Suppose that you lived in New Mexico during Spanish colonial times. How would your life be different from what it is today? In what ways might your life be similar to today?

2. What special problems do you think the Spanish pioneers faced in New Mexico? Which of these problems do you think were the hardest? Why?

3. Why have many of the old Spanish occupations disappeared today? How are these jobs done now?

6

CHANGES UNDER MEXICAN RULE

For centuries, Indian and Hispanic people lived side by side in New Mexico. Then, after 1821, a new people appeared. They were the Americans. They came from the East. Their country was growing and taking over new land. Soon, Americans were visiting and living in New Mexico. Now there were three cultures in New Mexico—the Indian, the Hispanic, and the American. Would the three cultures get along together? Only the future would tell.

independent

The year 1821 was important for New Mexico. It became part of an **independent** Mexico. The days of Spanish rule were over. Now the people of New Mexico called them-

The Santa Fe Trail

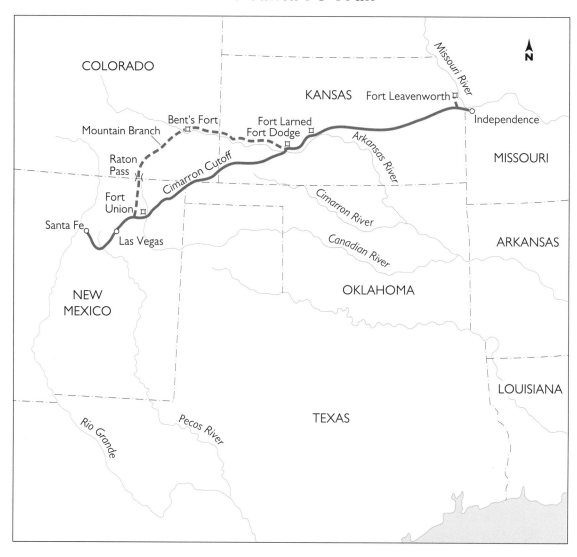

selves "Mexicans." They were proud of their new country.

Also in 1821, the Santa Fe Trail was opened. The trail connected New Mexico with the United States. In those days, the frontier of the United States lay far to the east in Missouri. In between were plains and mountains where only a few thousand Indians lived.

The 25 years of the Mexican period were a difficult time for New Mexico. The area had many problems. There was little money to help solve them. The new government far away in Mexico City could offer no aid.

In these years, Americans entered New Mexico in growing numbers. They brought new ideas. With them came new religious beliefs, new politics, and new customs. Life in New Mexico began to change.

William Becknell's first pack train over the Santa Fe Trail in 1821. *What kinds of problems did the early Santa Fe traders face during their journeys?*

frontier

A Celebration

News from Mexico City traveled slowly. People in Santa Fe did not learn of independence from Spain until late in 1821. The governor, Facundo Melgares, called a celebration. He set the date for January 6, 1822.

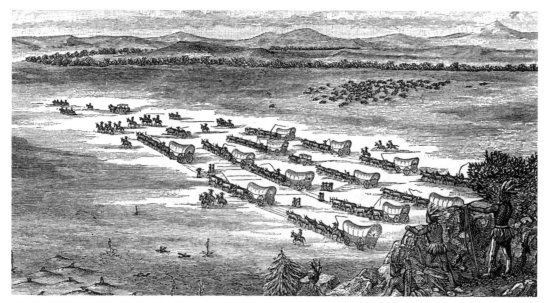

A wagon caravan traveling across New Mexico in the 1840s. *How is this picture like the one on page 125? How is it different?*

On that day people gathered in the Santa Fe plaza. There were speeches and songs. Soldiers fired cannons and shot rifles in the air. A tall tree trunk was raised in the plaza. On the pole waved the new flag of Mexico.

Opening the Santa Fe Trail

In the fall of 1821, William Becknell started across the plains from Missouri. Becknell was an American. With him was a group of **traders**. They had mules loaded with trade goods.

After many weeks, Becknell and his party reached Santa Fe. Governor Melgares welcomed them. He said Americans were now free to trade in New Mexico. The people of Santa Fe were eager to buy or trade for the things Becknell brought. Quickly the

traders

Americans finished their business. Then they headed home. They were happy with the money they had made.

The next year, 1822, Becknell returned to Santa Fe. This time he brought covered wagons. The wagons could carry more goods than mules alone. Becknell was the first to take wagons across the great plains. The heavy wagon wheels left deep tracks in the ground.

This is how the Santa Fe plaza looked in the days when it was the end of the trail. *How is the plaza different now?*

Other Americans soon followed Becknell's wagon tracks to New Mexico. The tracks became known as the Santa Fe Trail. The trail started in Independence, Missouri. It crossed the rolling plains of Kansas. In western Kansas the trail forked.

One fork went west into Colorado and crossed Raton Pass into New Mexico. The other fork went southwest across a corner of Oklahoma. Then it entered New Mexico north of present-day Clayton. Both forks came together again east of Las Vegas.

Becknell had opened the road that joined New Mexico to the United States. For that reason, he is called the "Father of the Santa Fe Trail."

Independence Square where the wagons started for Santa Fe.

Life on the Trail

How exciting it was to join a wagon train heading for New Mexico. Can you imagine it? Matt Field, a young newspaper reporter, told what it would be like at the start.

The wagons gather at Independence. Some are pulled by oxen, some by mules. Men shout orders to their helpers. There is much noise and color. Everyone is busy as the last boxes and barrels are loaded. When all is ready, the drivers pop their whips. Wagon wheels begin to turn. People in the street wave. They yell good-bye to friends who are leaving for Santa Fe.

The wagon train rolls out of Independence. It will take two months to make the 800-mile trip to Santa Fe. Many dangers lie ahead. There will be storms on the open plains. Deep rivers will have to be crossed. Pawnees, Comanches, and Kiowas may attack the wagons. Such a trip is only for the brave.

Though there were hardships, the traders came to love life on the trail. The air was crisp and sweet at dawn. Each sunrise, the sky turned bright red. The land stretched as far as a person could see. Fresh buffalo meat

Blizzards on the Plains

Travelers on the Santa Fe Trail were afraid of **blizzards**, or severe snow storms. Wind suddenly came howling from the north. Snow flew thick in the air. Temperatures dropped to zero or below.

No wagon train wanted to be caught in such a storm. On the open plains, a blizzard might easily kill the men and animals.

In 1842 Manuel Alvarez left Santa Fe for Missouri. It was late October. He and his men got caught in a snow storm.

"It lasted for 48 hours," wrote Mr. Alvarez. "The wind was so hard it blew out our fire. Snow fell three feet deep. We were all more or less frozen. Only one man died."

In later years, other caravans were hit by blizzards. The wagons were formed in a circle. This made a corral. Inside the circle, horses, mules, and oxen were driven for the night.

The men put up tents and went to bed. All night they could hear the sleet hitting the tent canvas. Often the heavy snow caused the tent to fall on the heads of the sleepers.

Next morning the people went out to look at the damage. Sometimes all of their animals had frozen to death overnight. Then they had to stay camped until help came. They would burn the wooden parts of the wagons to keep warm.

Crossing the Santa Fe Trail in winter was always dangerous. The traders avoided it if they could.

was roasted over campfires. When the wagons reached the mountains, there were streams running cold and clear.

But the best part of all came at the end of the trail. Everyone was eager to reach Santa Fe. Outside of town, the wagons stopped briefly. The traders and drivers put on clean shirts. They cut their hair and washed their faces. They wanted to look their best when they arrived in Santa Fe.

Finally, the wagons rolled into town. The people of Santa Fe smiled and waved. They

blizzard

In 1867, José Gurulé went east on the Santa Fe Trail to Missouri. He was 16 years old and traveled with the wagons owned by José Perea. Here, the boy tells of hardships on the trail:

We drove the wagons 18 hours a day. That left only 6 hours for sleep. We were always tired. Sometimes at noon we got a short nap. But the mules would begin braying and wake us up. We called the mules "alarm clocks." Once a man went to sleep and fell off a wagon. He was crushed by the wheels. We stopped only long enough to bury him. We got only one full meal each day. Then there were two light snacks. Each snack consisted of a tortilla and a raw onion eaten on the run. For a while we had sugar cubes brought in our pockets. Often we had to run beside the wagons to keep up.

called: *"Los Americanos! Los Americanos!"* The Americans had come all the way from Missouri with good things to sell.

Not all the traders stayed in Santa Fe. Some of them followed the old Camino Real south. They took their wagons to Albuquerque or El Paso. Many continued on to Chihuahua and other towns in Mexico. Thus, the Santa Fe trade spread far and wide across the land.

Josiah Gregg

One of the most famous traders was Josiah Gregg. As a young man, he was often sick. People then thought that life outdoors in the fresh air would cure almost anything.

Josiah's doctor told him to take a trip to Santa Fe. Maybe life on the trail would be a good medicine. And so it was! Josiah was sick when he left Independence in a wagon. But a week later, he was much better. He felt so good he climbed on a horse and went buffalo hunting!

By the end of the trip, Josiah Gregg was cured. He decided to become a Santa Fe trader. During the 1830s, he made many trips over the trail. He learned much about the trading business.

New Mexico was still a strange place for Americans. It lay in a foreign country—Mexico. The people spoke Spanish, not English. Americans were curious about New Mexico. They were interested in life on the Santa Fe Trail. They wanted to know more.

So, Josiah Gregg decided to write a book. He called it *Commerce of the Prairies*. This book told all about the wagon trains to Santa Fe. It told about the trail and watering places. And it told how to take care of the oxen and mules along the way.

Gregg's book also explained how people lived in New Mexico. For example, it said that many people rode burros instead of horses. A burro is a small Mexican donkey. The burro is very strong. It can carry heavy loads. Sometimes, says Gregg, a whole family rode on one burro. The father sat in the back. The mother rode in the middle. The children rode up front.

Josiah Gregg, author of *Commerce of the Prairies*.

burros

Burros in Santa Fe about 1890.

Commerce of the Prairies was very popular. Many Americans read it. It is still one of the best books on New Mexico and the Santa Fe Trail.

The New Mexican Traders

Americans were not the only ones who traveled the Santa Fe Trail. New Mexicans wanted part of the business, too. The Armijo, Baca, Perea, Chávez, Otero, and other families formed their own wagon trains. They crossed the prairies to Missouri. They bought goods cheaply and carried them back to New Mexico to be sold.

The New Mexicans made a lot of money. They were good at business. Within a few years, some of them were rich. José Perea of Bernalillo and Felipe Chávez of Belen became very rich. They were among the richest men in New Mexico.

The Mountain Men

Fur trappers entered the Southwest during the Mexican period. They were men who trapped beaver for their fur. In the United States, beaver fur was used to make hats. The fur was very expensive. Trappers could make a lot of money at this work.

These trappers were called mountain men. They lived in the mountains for months at a time. That was where the beaver could be found. The mountain men were tough. They dressed in leather clothes and some wore long beards.

Indians, like the Utes, often attacked

THE OLD TRAPPER.

Mountain men like this hunted beaver along New Mexico's streams and rivers. *Why did they wear the buckskin clothing?*

fur trapper

fandango

them. The Utes did not want the trappers in their country. So the mountain men always had to look out for danger.

At least once a year, the mountain men rode to Taos, at the foot of the Rockies. They came to sell their furs. But they also came to have a good time. Once in Taos, they could forget the dangers of the mountains. In Taos there was good food to eat. They could also enjoy the exciting dances called **fandangos**.

At a fandango, the mountain men danced and danced. They clapped and sang. They yelled and fired their guns in the air. They also drank a strong whisky called Taos Lightning. Many times, the fandango ended with a fight. The mountain men were used to the wilderness. Many of them had forgotten how to behave when they came to town.

Bent's Fort

In the 1830s, two brothers built an adobe fort. The brothers were Charles and William Bent. This fort was in Colorado, on the mountain branch of the Santa Fe Trail. The mountain branch was the fork that went over Raton Pass.

Bent's Fort was in Colorado. But it played an important part in New Mexico history. The Bent brothers sold goods to travelers on the trail. They bought beaver skins from the

Bent's Fort is in southeastern Colorado. It was rebuilt by the Park Service in the 1960s. *Why was Bent's Fort important to the region of New Mexico and Colorado?*

trappers and traded buffalo robes from the Plains Indians.

Charles Bent had a home and store in Taos. He spent much of his time there and in Santa Fe. Charles Bent and his brother were very important in New Mexico business.

Kit Carson

One of the best-known trappers was Kit Carson. As a boy, he lived in Franklin, Missouri. That was near the start of the Santa Fe Trail. He worked in a saddle shop for a man named Mr. Workman. But Kit was eager for adventure.

One day in 1826, he ran away. He joined a wagon train going to Santa Fe. Mr. Workman put an ad in the paper. He offered to pay a

Changes Under Mexican Rule

Christopher "Kit" Carson.

reward of one penny. The penny would go to anyone bringing the boy Kit back to his job in the saddle shop. Clearly, Mr. Workman did not think much of Kit if he would pay only a penny for his return.

But young Kit Carson had found a new life in the West. From Santa Fe, he went to Taos. There he joined a party of mountain men leaving for the wilderness. Soon he learned all about beaver. He learned the best way to trap them. He was now a mountain man himself.

Yet Kit was not like the other mountain men. The hard life in the Rockies did not make him wild. He did not drink whisky or shoot up the fandangoes. Instead, he wanted a quiet home and a family.

In 1843, Kit married Josefa Jaramillo of Taos. Her sister Maria was married to Charles Bent. So now Kit and Charles were brothers-in-law. Kit and Josefa had a nice adobe house near the Taos plaza. That house is still standing. Today it is a museum honoring Kit Carson.

Troubles Begin

At first, the Mexican government had welcomed Americans. It let them trade, trap, and settle in New Mexico, Texas, and California. But soon Mexico began to fear the Americans.

When I was seven years old, about the year 1841, I was placed in the Beginner's School at Santa Fe. I would take a short cut to school across a barley field. Governor Manuel Armijo owned the field.

One day the Governor caught and hit me with his cane. He told me never to come that way again because it was not a public road. Even though I was scared and hurt from the blow of his cane, I knelt down and asked his blessing. Such were the orders of my teacher—always to ask our elders to bless us.

Governor Armijo then asked who my father was and where I was going. I replied: "I'm going to school, and my father is Don Albino Chacón."

Then he said: "Well, so you are a child of my good friend, Don Albino. Here, take this coin and cross my field whenever you wish."

From that day on, I always watched for the governor in his field. Whenever I saw him, I would go straight to where he was, kneel down, and ask his blessing. He always gave me another coin.

—from the Memoirs of Rafael
    Chacón, written in 1906

Manuel Armijo, the last governor of the Mexican period.
What kind of problems did he encounter as he tried to defend New Mexico?

General Stephen Kearny added New Mexico to the United States in 1846.

The United States was pushing its frontier west. Mexico was afraid of losing land along its northern border. In fact, that began to happen. In 1836, Americans in Texas started a war with Mexico. They set up the independent Republic of Texas.

New Mexico was really worried. Would New Mexico be lost next? In 1841, to make matters worse, Texas sent a small army toward Santa Fe. That army hoped to make New Mexico part of Texas. But this plan failed.

Governor Manuel Armijo at Santa Fe got his soldiers together. He marched east toward the plains. When the Texan army arrived at Anton Chico, he captured it. For the moment, anyway, New Mexico was safe. But for how long?

The Mexican government continued to say that Texas still belonged to Mexico. Then, late in 1845, the Republic of Texas joined the United States. War between Mexico and the United States soon followed. In history, it is called the Mexican War.

The Conquest of New Mexico

In the summer of 1846, General Stephen W. Kearny started west over the Santa Fe Trail. He was in charge of many soldiers and

A soldier with General Kearny in 1846 tells what he saw at a village north of Santa Fe:

The people here help each other through the busiest seasons. They were bringing in the wheat while we were there. After being cut and tied in bundles, it is spread over a clay threshing floor in the open air. Upon it are men with crude pitchforks, made of limbs of small trees. They throw the straw into the air as oxen trample out the grain. The straw, by this means, is broken up very fine. The wheat, after being collected, is carefully washed by the women and children, and then spread upon cloths to dry.

cannons. President James K. Polk had ordered him to **occupy**, or take control of, New Mexico and California.

Kearny followed the mountain branch of the trail. He stopped at Bent's Fort to rest his men. Then he headed for Las Vegas, New Mexico. This was the first New Mexican town occupied. There, General Kearny made a speech. He told the people that New Mexico was now part of the United States. He then promised to protect their lives, property, and religion. Not all newcomers followed his promises. Abuses occurred against New Mexicans. Some Hispanics even died in defense of their lives and property. Hostility quickly built up against some American officials and eventually split over into revolt.

Kearny and his men then continued west across the Pecos River. They climbed Glorieta Pass, and on August 18 they

occupy

entered Santa Fe. They occupied the town without firing a shot. Governor Armijo and his soldiers had fled to Mexico. So northern New Mexico was occupied peacefully.

At once General Kearny set up a new government. He made Charles Bent the first American governor. Bent spoke Spanish and had a home in Taos. Kearny thought the New Mexicans would accept him as governor. The general was soon proved wrong.

Next, Kearny divided his army. He sent one part down the Rio Grande under Colonel Alexander Doniphan. At Brazito, near Las Cruces, Colonel Doniphan fought a battle with Mexican soldiers. It took place on Christmas Day, 1846, and the Americans won. El Paso was captured next. Then Colonel Doniphan and his army marched on to Chihuahua.

General Kearny led the second part of his army to California. Kit Carson served as guide. Later, Kearny occupied California and added it to the United States.

The Revolt in Taos

When Kearny went to California, he left some soldiers to guard Santa Fe. Important men among the New Mexicans began to plan a revolt. They hoped to defeat the few Americans. They wanted to return their province to Mexican rule. They also wanted to take revenge against Americans they felt had wronged them. Their main target became the territorial governor, Charles Bent.

The Americans learned about the plans for the revolt. They arrested the leaders in Santa Fe. That seemed to put an end to the trouble.

But fighting broke out in Taos on January 19, 1847. Indians from Taos Pueblo joined with the local people to attack Governor Bent's house. They knocked down the door and shot Charles Bent full of arrows. Then they scalped him. His wife Maria and her sister Josefa (Kit Carson's wife) were also in the house with their children. But they were not harmed.

When the soldiers at Santa Fe heard of Bent's death, they hurried north. The rebels went inside the large church at Taos Pueblo. It had thick adobe walls and made a good fort.

For several hours, army troops and the Taos Indians fought a battle. The Americans fired cannon balls at the door. When the door blew open, they rushed in fighting. The rebels were defeated. Their leaders were

Ruins of the old church at Taos. It was destroyed by American soldiers in the battle of 1847.

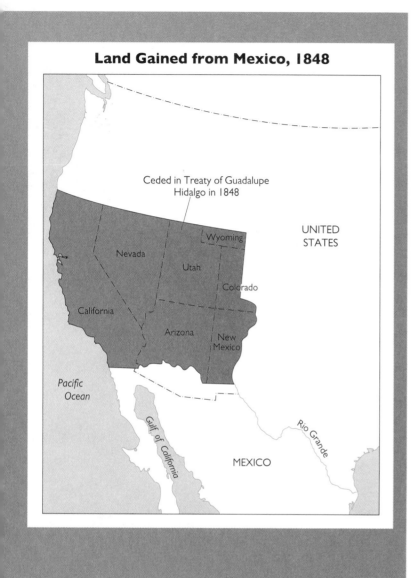

Land Gained from Mexico, 1848

Ceded in Treaty of Guadalupe
Hidalgo in 1848

UNITED
STATES

Wyoming

Nevada

Utah

Colorado

California

Arizona

New
Mexico

Pacific
Ocean

Gulf of California

Rio Grande

MEXICO

captured and later hanged. That was the end of the revolt.

The Peace Treaty

Following the trouble in Taos, New Mexico remained quiet. But other American soldiers continued the war against Mexico. Eventually they captured Mexico City and the Mexican War came to an end in February 1848.

With the fighting over, the United States and Mexico signed a peace treaty. It was called the Treaty of Guadalupe Hidalgo. For the United States, the land gained in 1848 later became the states of New Mexico, California, Nevada, Utah, Arizona, and parts of Wyoming and Colorado. It said that the private lands of the New Mexicans would be protected. Those were the lands given as grants by Spain and Mexico.

A New Time

After the war, the New Mexicans were worried. They knew that more changes were coming. But they did not know what kind. Now Americans were in control. They spoke English, and they had different laws. Their ways of work and play were not like those in New Mexico. These *Anglos,* as they were called, seemed to have new ideas about everything.

For example, the Anglos looked at land in a different way. To them, land was like any other property. It was just something to be bought and sold.

To the Hispanos (that is, the Spanish-speaking people), land was something more. Land was part of the family or part of the community.

Under American law, the Hispanos had to prove their land rights in court. Often the people had lost their old grant papers. They could not prove that they owned the land. Other times, Anglos and some Hispanos cheated the people out of their land. Over the years, the New Mexicans lost much of their land.

Even so, they kept their Hispanic culture. They kept their language and religion. And with all the changes in this new time, they kept their pride.

Anglos
Hispanos

Words to Know

Anglo	fandango	Hispano
blizzard	frontier	independent
burro	fur trapper	occupy
		trader

Reviewing What You Have Read

1. What country took over rule of New Mexico beginning in 1821?
2. Why is Becknell called the "Father of the Santa Fe Trail"?
3. How did the Santa Fe Trail help the city of Santa Fe?
4. What was Josiah Gregg's contribution to New Mexico?
5. Tell five hardships of life on the Santa Fe Trail.
6. Tell about the life of a mountain man.
7. What was the issue in the Mexican War? What countries fought the war?
8. Who was the first American governor in New Mexico? How did he become governor?
9. What was the result of the Treaty of Guadalupe Hidalgo?
10. What was one difficult change for Hispanos under the new United States rule?

For Thought and Discussion

1. Compare and contrast life under Mexican rule with life during the Spanish colonial period. During which period would you have liked to live? Why?

2. How do you think your life would be different today if Mexico had won the Mexican War?

3. In what ways did the traders and the mountain men prepare the way for modern New Mexico?

7

TERRITORIAL DAYS

War is a terrible thing. It destroys lives. It brings down nations. Wars change the direction of history. They did much to change the direction of history in New Mexico. In the early days of the New Mexico Territory, many wars were fought. War cast its dark shadow all across the land.

From 1847 to 1850, the American army ruled in New Mexico. That was because officials in Washington could not decide what to do. Should they make New Mexico a territory? Or should they let New Mexico become a state at once?

A territory was land not yet ready to become a state. Not many people lived there. The governor and other officials were not

official

territory

James S. Calhoun, New Mexico's first territorial governor, appointed in 1850. He served one year.

statehood
census

elected by the people. They were given their jobs by the president. When a territory had 60,000 people, it could become a state.

New Mexico presented a special problem. By 1850, it had almost 60,000 people. It would soon be able to become a state. But some members of Congress were against this. They said that most people in New Mexico did not speak English. They did not understand the laws or voting process of the United States. These members of Congress believed New Mexico should remain a territory until education had prepared the people for statehood.

So, New Mexico was made into a territory in 1850. Most citizens were unhappy about that. They thought New Mexico should become a state as soon as possible. But many years would pass before statehood was won.

A New Governor

James S. Calhoun became the first governor of the New Mexico Territory. As governor, he faced many problems. A territorial government had to be set up. There was no money to pay expenses. A census was needed, to learn how many people lived in New Mexico. But the chief problem was the war with the Indians.

After the Americans had come, troubles with the Apaches and Navajos got worse.

Those tribes were fighting hard to keep their homeland. They attacked wagon trains and towns along the Rio Grande. Governor Calhoun wrote the president about this. He said there would be no peace in New Mexico until both the Apaches and Navajos were defeated. Yet, peace was far in the future.

James S. Calhoun worked hard to put the territorial government in order. But his health was poor. After a year in office, he learned he was dying. He decided to return to his home in the East. Before joining a wagon train, he had a coffin made to take with him. The governor did not want to die on the Santa Fe Trail without a coffin.

Sure enough, in the middle of Kansas Governor Calhoun died. His body was taken to Kansas City, Missouri, to be buried. Calhoun served New Mexico only a year. But he helped the new territory get a good start.

Settling New Mexico's Borders

In 1850, the New Mexico Territory was much larger than our state today. It stretched all the way to California. All of Arizona and part of Southern Colorado were part of New Mexico. In time, the territory was reshaped to form the state as we know it now.

Working out the southern border with Mexico caused the biggest problem. After the Mexican War, a new line had to be drawn between the United States and Mexico. Neither country could agree where the line should be. And both claimed the Mesilla Valley.

The Mesilla Valley, just above El Paso, had good farmland. The few towns, like Doña Ana and Mesilla, were small. But one day this would be a rich and valuable area. Here Las Cruces would develop as New Mexico's second largest city.

For a while, it seemed war might break out again over the Mesilla Valley. Finally, the matter was settled. The United States government sent James Gadsden to Mexico to work out a deal. He offered Mexico $10 million for the valley and for a strip of desert to the west. This was known as the Gadsden Purchase. It established New Mexico's border with Mexico.

In 1861, Colorado became a territory. At that time, part of northeastern New Mexico was added to Colorado. New Mexicans had recently moved north and settled in the San Luis Valley and around Trinidad. Now they became citizens of Colorado.

One more major change was yet to come. In 1863, Congress carved a new territory out of western New Mexico. The territory was called Arizona. With that, New Mexico's modern borders were complete.

Soldiers at Fort Stanton line up on the parade ground.
What important services did the army provide the residents of New Mexico?

Military Forts

The United States government built many new forts in New Mexico to protect travelers and settlers. The army bought crops from local farmers to feed the soldiers. It also bought hay and firewood. The forts helped New Mexico's economy.

There were several army posts along the Rio Grande. Fort Craig near Socorro and Forts Fillmore and Selden in the Mesilla Valley were the most important. Fort Cummings, north of Deming, was built to protect miners and passing stagecoaches. Fort Stanton was established in 1855 in the Mescalero Apache country. Later, the army

U.S. Forts in New Mexico

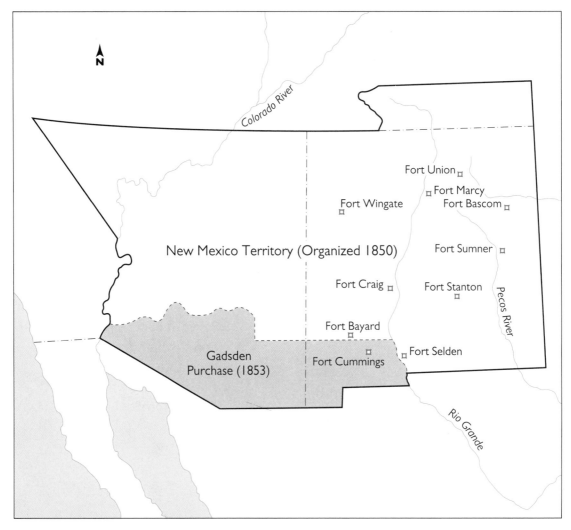

Ruins of old Fort Selden in the Mesilla Valley. *What was the purpose of Fort Selden?*

founded Fort Sumner on the Pecos River and Fort Bascom on the plains near Tucumcari.

Fort Union, begun in 1851, was New Mexico's most important army post. Its main duty was to guard the western end of the Santa Fe Trail. It was also used to store supplies. Army supplies were brought to the fort by wagon. Later, the supplies were sent to forts around the Southwest.

Today, Fort Union is a national monument. There, visitors can see ruins of the fort. Grass-covered ruts of the Santa Fe Trail are still plain. A museum helps explain what life was like for the soldiers. Visiting Fort Union is a good way to learn about territorial New Mexico.

The Civil War Begins

The Civil War was one of the most bloody wars in our nation's history. It was fought mainly in the East between the Northern states and the Southern states. Slavery was the major issue.

The people of the South bought and sold slaves. They used slave labor on their cotton plantations. The Northern states, which had no plantations, did not allow slavery. Many people there thought it should be abolished, or ended. Such Northerners were called **abolitionists.**

Abraham Lincoln was elected president in 1860. He was against slavery. The Southern states decided to break away from the United States. They set up a new country called the Confederate States of America. Sometimes it was called simply "The Confederacy."

President Lincoln was not willing to let the Southern states break away. He said that would destroy the nation. The rebels of the South must be stopped. So, the Civil War began.

New Mexico was far away from the main battle area. There were very few black slaves in the territory. However, there were several hundred Indian slaves. These were mostly **captive** Apaches and Navajos. Most New Mexicans did not believe a war should he fought over slavery. They wanted to stay out of the war. But that became impossible.

Don Santiago Hubbell was a volunteer from New Mexico during the Civil War. *How does the uniform of this Civil War soldier differ from that worn by soldiers today?*

The Confederate Invasion

The new Confederate States needed money to fight the war. Most of all, they needed gold to buy guns in Europe. Both Colorado and California had plenty of gold mines. The Confederates wanted to seize those mines. Then they would have plenty of gold to help them in the war. First, however, New Mexico had to be occupied. The roads to the Colorado and California gold fields passed through New Mexico.

Texas, one of the Confederate States, sent soldiers to take New Mexico. From El Paso came Colonel John R. Baylor and 300 Texans. They captured Fort Fillmore and the town of Mesilla. Baylor created the Confederate Territory of Arizona and made Mesilla the capital. This territory took in southern New Mexico and southern Arizona.

Another Confederate army arrived at Mesilla in February of 1862. It was led by General Henry H. Sibley. These Texans soon began marching up the Rio Grande.

Ahead stood Fort Craig. At the fort were regular army troops and New Mexico **volunteers**. The volunteers were citizens who had agreed to help defend New Mexico. The commander was Colonel Edward Canby. Kit Carson was there, too. He was the head of some of the volunteers.

Sibley's Confederates tried to cross the Rio

General Henry H. Sibley led a Confederate army from Texas in 1862. He tried, but failed, to conquer New Mexico for the South. *Why did Sibley's invasion fail?*

abolitionist
captive
volunteer

Two of the army units that patrolled the frontier were made up of black soldiers:

The troopers of the Ninth and Tenth Regiments, comprising about 20 percent of the U.S. Cavalry in the West, soon achieved an outstanding record on the frontier. These black troopers won the respect of every military friend or foe they encountered. Their Indian adversaries, intrigued by their short, curled hair, and comparing them to an animal they considered sacred, called them the "Buffalo Soldiers."

During the last frontier days, eleven black soldiers earned the nation's highest military decoration, the Medal of Honor. The earliest recipient was Emanuel Stance, a sergeant in Company F. Ninth Cavalry.

—William Loren Katz, The Black West

Buffalo Soldiers camped near Chloride, New Mexico about 1892.

Grande at Valverde a few miles from the fort. Colonel Canby sent his men to stop them. The Battle of Valverde took place at the crossing. It was the first major battle of the Civil War in the Southwest.

The fighting lasted several hours. Men were killed and wounded on both sides. The Confederate forces won, but they failed to capture Fort Craig.

The Civil War in New Mexico, 1861–1862

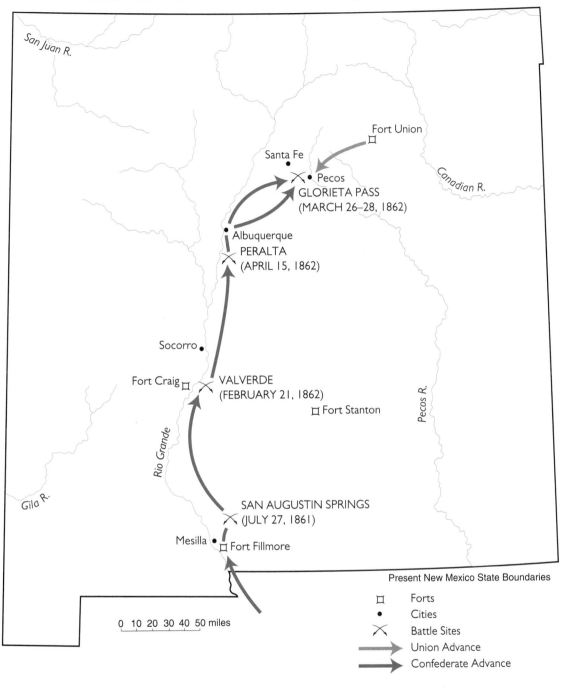

San Juan R.

Canadian R.

Fort Union

Santa Fe

Pecos

GLORIETA PASS
(MARCH 26–28, 1862)

Albuquerque

PERALTA
(APRIL 15, 1862)

Socorro

Fort Craig

VALVERDE
(FEBRUARY 21, 1862)

Fort Stanton

Pecos R.

Rio Grande

Gila R.

SAN AUGUSTIN SPRINGS
(JULY 27, 1861)

Mesilla

Fort Fillmore

0 10 20 30 40 50 miles

Present New Mexico State Boundaries

Forts
Cities
Battle Sites
Union Advance
Confederate Advance

The Battle of Glorieta Pass was fought here, on Pigeon's Ranch. *Why was this battle important to New Mexico and the Union?*

After the battle, General Sibley continued his march north. Soon the Confederate flag flew over the plazas in Albuquerque and Santa Fe. It seemed New Mexico would be lost by the United States.

Help was on the way, however. Colorado volunteers rode over Raton Pass. These volunteers were on the side of the North. They reached Fort Union and joined the troops there. The volunteers were called "Pike's Peakers," because they came from the goldfields near Pike's Peak.

In late March, the Pike's Peakers and Fort Union soldiers marched to Glorieta Pass east of Santa Fe. There they met the Confederate army. The Battle of Glorieta was the turning point of the war in the West.

Colonel Manuel Chaves was chief scout. While the battle was going on, he carried out a dangerous mission. He led 430 of the Pike's Peakers over a secret trail on Glorieta Mesa. Chaves and his men got behind the Confederate line. They burned General Sibley's wagon train of supplies.

Burning of the wagon train forced the Confederates to leave New Mexico. They no longer had food or extra bullets to carry on the fight. For New Mexico, the Civil War was over.

A Confederate soldier's description of the battle of Glorieta:

The battle began at an early hour in the morning. The enemy made an attack on our right, left, and front. Our boys charged up the high cliffs on both sides of the line. That brought on a hand-to-hand fight with the enemy who occupied the heights.

The conflict was desperate. Few of our men stopped to reload after firing. They used their guns as clubs. For two hours the battle raged with fury. The enemy fought with determination. Yelling, our little army drove them back inches at a time.

We were determined to do or die and finally broke their lines. That night snow fell near one foot deep. Many of the wounded died from the cold. The brave men who fought there deserve much from their country.

—Theo Noel, 4th Texas Cavalry, CSA

During the battle of Glorieta Pass, Union soldiers burned the Confederate supply train. *Why did the burning of the supply train ensure victory for the Union army?*

The old Albuquerque Plaza as it might have looked at the time of the Civil War.

The plaza in old Mesilla, one of the earliest towns in southern New Mexico.
Does your town have a plaza?

The Last Indian Wars

During the Confederate invasion, Indian raids in the territory grew in number. The white people were fighting among themselves. So, the tribes decided it was a good time to strike. The Apaches and Navajos attacked on one side. The Comanches and Kiowas attacked from the other.

In 1862, General James Carleton came to New Mexico with an army of volunteers from California. Like the Pike's Peakers from Colorado, these men hoped to fight the Confederates. But they arrived too late. Sibley's Texans had already left.

General Carleton became the head of the army in New Mexico. With his California volunteers, he began to make war against the Indians. He believed in harsh punishment. He said to his soldiers: "All Indian men are to be killed wherever you find them. The women and children will not be harmed, but you will take them prisoners."

The Mescalero Apache War

Late in 1862 General Carleton sent Kit Carson to defeat the Mescaleros. These Apaches lived in the mountains between the present-day towns of Roswell and Alamogordo. This was forest country with rushing streams. The hunting was good here. Some of the Mescaleros roamed the Guadalupe

invasion

Mountains. Those mountains stretch south into Texas.

Carson and his men chased the Mescaleros through the winter. By spring, the Apaches were defeated. About 400 Apache families were taken to a new reservation called Bosque Redondo. It lay on the Pecos River next to Fort Sumner.

The Navajos and the Long Walk

For centuries, the Navajos fought the Spaniards. Later they fought the Americans just as hard. This tribe lived in western New Mexico and the deserts of eastern Arizona. They raised sheep for meat and wool. The Navajos grew corn and peach trees in some of the far canyons.

After the defeat of the Mescaleros, General Carleton ordered Kit Carson to march against the Navajos. But Carson was not eager to go on fighting the Indians. He asked Carleton to give someone else the job. The general, however, ordered him to do his duty. With that, Kit Carson agreed.

The last Navajo war continued through 1863. There were no major battles. But Carson's men captured most of the Navajos' sheep and horses. They burned the crops and cut down hundreds of peach trees. The

reservation

The Navajo people have their own history of the captivity at Fort Sumner (Bosque Redondo) and the Long Walk. Here, a Navajo man tells part of the story as he heard it from his grandparents:

At Fort Sumner, each Diné [Navajo] would be given one slice of bread. At times they would kill a rabbit or a rat. If a rat was killed, the meat with the bones and intestines would be chopped into pieces. Twelve persons would share it.

Finally the commanding officer asked the Diné if they really missed their country. The Diné responded noisily, "Yes, we miss our country very much and would like to go back." Soon after that, they were set free and walked back to Arizona. There they were issued some sheep.

After the Diné returned from Fort Sumner, they started thinking about living better lives.

—Account of Mose Denejolie

Picture of Geronimo, most famous of all Apaches, in the days when he was fighting against the U.S. Army.
Why was he a great Indian leader?

tribe could find no rest or safety anywhere.

Kit Carson did not obey Carleton's order to kill all the Indian men. By summer of 1864, about 8,000 Navajos had given up. They were sent east to the Bosque Redondo Reservation. It was a long way and the Indians had to walk. Many Navajos died from the hardships of the trip.

For the next four years, the tribe suffered at its new home on the Pecos River. There were quarrels with their old enemies, the Mescaleros. But soon the Mescaleros slipped away and returned to their mountains in the south.

The food was bad at Bosque Redondo. The water was salty and there was no grass for the livestock. There was little firewood. Many of the captives grew sick and died. All the people hoped for the day when they could return to their own country. This was a sad time in Navajo history. It was a time never to be forgotten.

At last, in 1868, the government agreed to let the Navajos go home. There were wagons for some. But again most people walked the whole way. The trip was always remembered by the tribe as the "Long Walk."

After many days, the tribe reached Albuquerque. From there they could see Mount Taylor, 60 miles away. In the Navajo language it was called Tso Dzil. It was a holy mountain, home of Turquoise Boy and Yellow Corn Girl. People began to cry when they saw Tso Dzil. They knew their homeland was just beyond. The Long Walk would soon be over.

Peace At Last

For a while, the war with other tribes went on. Soldiers from Fort Union and Fort Bascom chased the Comanches and Kiowas across the plains. By 1874, both tribes made peace. They went to reservations in the Indian Territory (now called Oklahoma).

In the north, the Utes and Jicarilla Apaches were defeated. The Utes were sent to a reservation in Colorado. But the Jicarillas were given a large reservation in far northern New Mexico. There they could begin raising cattle. They could start making a new life for themselves.

The Chiricahua Apache in southern New Mexico fought the longest. Many books have been written about their fight. Many stories have been told about their famous leaders, such as Cochise, Mangas Coloradas (Red Sleeves), Victorio, and Geronimo.

Geronimo was the last to give up, in 1886. In fact he was the last Indian to surrender to the United States Government.

Silversmithing has been an important occupation for the Navajo people. This photo is of an early Navajo silversmith showing his tools and jewelry.

Manuel Chaves and his wife, Vicenta.

Manuel Chaves, Pioneer and Soldier

History is the story of individual people. One of the most interesting persons of this period was Manuel Chaves. He was the scout who played a part in the battle of Glorieta.

Chaves did many other things. His life was filled with adventure and danger. He did not believe in sitting still.

Little Manuel was born in 1818, while New Mexico belonged to Spain. Three years later, independence came and he grew up under the flag of Mexico. His later life was spent in the territory as an American citizen.

Living his whole life on the frontier, Manuel had a role in the major events of his day. At different times, he was a rancher, army scout, and leader of military troops. Kit Carson was his friend.

Like Kit Carson, Chaves was very small in size. But many brave men and women have been small. Friends called Manuel Chaves *El Leoncito.* That means "The Little Lion." He was small, but he was as brave as a lion.

Willa Cather wrote a famous book on New Mexico, called *Death Comes for the Archbishop.* In it, she told about Manuel Chaves. She said he was "a handsome man with a passion for danger." Willa Cather never met Manuel. But she learned all about him from Manuel's son, Amado.

Manuel Chaves died on his ranch near Grants in 1889. By then, New Mexico was very different from the land he had known as a boy. There were signs of progress everywhere. More than 160,000 people now lived in the territory. Manuel Chaves was one of those who helped lead New Mexico toward the modern age.

Words to Know

abolitionist   invasion   statehood

captive   official   territory

census   reservation   volunteer

Reviewing What You Have Read

1. What is a territory?
2. Who was the first governor of the New Mexico Territory?
3. What was the Gadsden Purchase?
4. Why did a Confederate army from Texas invade New Mexico in 1862?
5. Who were the Pike's Peakers?
6. How did Colonel Manuel Chaves stop the Confederate army?
7. What did General Carleton tell his soldiers to do to all Indian men?
8. What was life like for the Navajos at Bosque Redondo?
9. For the Navajos in 1868, what was the "Long Walk"?
10. Who was Geronimo?

For Thought and Discussion

1. The New Mexico Territory in 1850 was much larger than our state is today. Why do you think the territory was made smaller?

2. Why do you think the Mexican government agreed to the Gadsden Purchase? What might have happened if Mexico had not agreed?

3. Suppose you had been a Navajo on the Long Walk. How would you have felt about the way you had been treated? How would you have felt when you finally got back home?

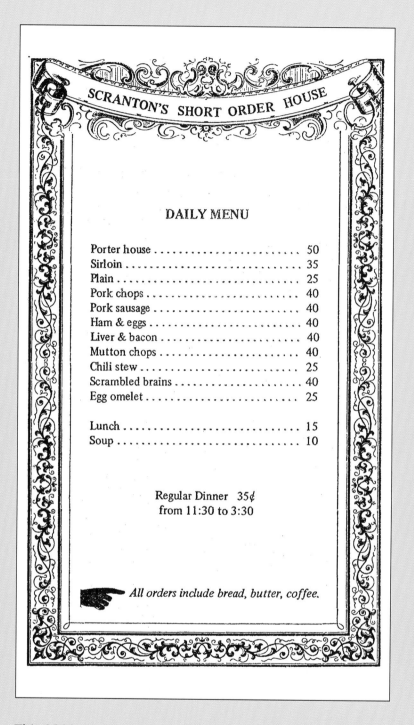

DAILY MENU

Porter house	50
Sirloin	35
Plain	25
Pork chops	40
Pork sausage	40
Ham & eggs	40
Liver & bacon	40
Mutton chops	40
Chili stew	25
Scrambled brains	40
Egg omelet	25
Lunch	15
Soup	10

Regular Dinner 35¢
from 11:30 to 3:30

All orders include bread, butter, coffee.

SCRANTON'S SHORT ORDER HOUSE

This 1890 menu from the mining town of Cerrillos shows how prices have changed. *How is this menu different from one you might see today?*

8
LIFE IN THE TERRITORY

For many years New Mexico was a frontier territory. New people arrived by wagon and stagecoach. Later, they came by railroad. They settled the land and built new towns. Little by little, the frontier disappeared. New Mexico moved forward on the road of progress.

In the territorial period, the Hispanos were not pushed aside. True, many lost their lands. But there were many more Spanish-speaking people than Anglos. In the early years, the few Anglos had to learn Spanish. Without it, they could not do business or talk to their neighbors.

Many Hispanos served in the territorial

Becoming Americanized. A young Hispano of the 1880s in Anglo-style clothes and haircut.

Americanized
lumbering

government. Both English and Spanish were used as official languages. Also, government documents were printed in the two languages.

Even so, New Mexico slowly became **Americanized**. The new American settlers were builders and developers. They had come to New Mexico to make money. They were interested in the future, not the past. The old way of life was not so important to them.

After the Civil War, new towns sprang up around New Mexico. The government built new roads for wagons and stagecoaches. Later, railroads reached the territory. Ranching and farming grew. Mining and **lumbering** also became more important. Changes could be seen everywhere.

It was a time when schools and churches were started. People arriving wanted a good environment for their children. But it was also a time of outlaws. Famous outlaws made New Mexico their home. They made life hard for peaceful citizens.

Growth of Towns and Cities

New Mexico's oldest towns got their start in the Spanish and Mexican periods. Santa Fe began in 1610. Other places, like Taos, Bernalillo, Albuquerque, Belen, and Socorro were founded after the Pueblo Revolt. These and smaller towns were in north-central New Mexico.

Only later, after the Indian wars were over, did people settle on the east and west sides. Hispanos from the Rio Grande Valley led the way. With their sheep, they moved across the Staked Plains. Some built towns as far east as the Texas Panhandle. Others went west. They settled along the Arizona border or in the San Juan Basin.

Many new towns grew from farming and ranching centers. Roswell, Artesia, and Farmington are towns like these. Other places began as important points on the new railroads. Raton, Clovis, Tucumcari, Santa Rosa, Alamogordo, and Deming are such towns.

Finally, many small mining camps grew into important towns. But after the mines closed, these places became ghost towns. Mogollon, Kingston, Shakespeare, White Oaks, and Lake Valley are famous ghost towns of New Mexico. On the other hand, Silver City remained an important mining town. It is now a major supply center for southwestern New Mexico.

Rural Development

During the territorial days, towns and cities in New Mexico grew. Many people moved to the cities from rural, or country,

ghost town
rural

John Chisum. *Why is he significant to New Mexico history?*

areas. But most people continued to live in the rural areas. They farmed. Or they took care of their cattle and sheep.

This was the period when huge cattle ranches appeared. By 1880, the buffalo were gone from the plains. So cattle could take their place. A few people developed great ranching empires in the plains, mountains, and deserts of New Mexico.

One successful rancher was John Chisum. He owned thousands of cattle. His ranch lay on the Pecos River near Roswell. It was on the old Goodnight-Loving cattle trail that ran from Texas north to Colorado. Chisum was known as the "Cow King of New Mexico." For a while in the 1870s, he was the most successful rancher in the United States.

Others made good money from raising sheep. Their flocks numbered in the thousands. For years, Solomon Luna owned the largest sheep ranch in the territory. He was so rich and powerful that people called him "King Sol." In 1912, he fell into a vat of sheep dip and drowned.

Mining gold, silver, copper, lead, and turquoise was also important. Miners worked for low pay, often under terrible conditions. Lumbering, too, grew much more important. Trees were cut, not only for lumber, but for railroad ties and fence posts.

Cowboy Ways

Cowboy life in New Mexico and other western states is often pictured in books and movies. Cowboys had a hard job. They needed special skills to take care of cattle. Every day they faced danger and hardship. They rode bucking horses and roped wild steers. The cowboy became a symbol of America's Wild West.

Eugene Manlove Rhodes learned to be a cowboy at a young age. He worked for large ranches in the Tularosa Basin of central New Mexico. Later, he wrote many famous stories about cowboy life. One of his best known books is *Paso Por Aquí*.

Cowboy ways in New Mexico were borrowed from Spain and Mexico. They included clothes: a big hat, or sombrero; boots; and chaps. Equipment: lariat, branding iron, and big spurs. Horse colors: pinto and palomino. And even words were borrowed. *Rancho, corral*, and *wrangler* all come from Spanish.

The 1860s and 1870s was the Golden Age of the cowboy. As yet there were no fences.

Workers in front of their mine near White Oaks. *What dangers did miners face?*

Agnes Morley Cleaveland grew up on a cattle ranch in western New Mexico. Here, she recalls the early days:

As youngsters we learned to recognize the individuals among the cattle as though they had been people. How well I remember them coming in to the watering trough, bellowing and flipping their tails. We watched for their coming with the same interest we would have had in the arrival of personal friends.

Twice a year roundups were held. In spring it was to brand the new calf crop. In fall the cattle were sent to market or directly to the laughter-houses in Chicago.

It was always occasion for deep heartache when we children saw our friends set forth on their last journey. But it was part of life and we had to face it.

—from *No Life for a Lady*

The range was open and free to everyone.

Ranchers built cattle empires. With their cowboys they went on long trail drives. The cattle were rounded up and driven for many weeks to market. One of the routes was the Goodnight-Loving Trail. It ran from west Texas up the Pecos River to Fort Sumner, New Mexico and beyond.

An early New Mexico cowboy was George McJunkin. Remember, he was the man who helped discover the famous Folsom points. McJunkin was black and an ex-slave from Texas. He became known as a good cowhand and bronc rider.

In time McJunkin became foreman of the

Crowfoot Ranch. He won the respect of all who knew him.

One day the foreman went to town. He stopped for supper at a cafe where cowboys ate. Soon an Easterner came in. The stranger saw McJunkin sitting at a table. He told the cafe owner to throw him out because he didn't want to sit with a black man.

Instead, the cowboys grabbed the stranger and tossed him out the front door into a mud puddle. They would not share the cafe with someone who was **prejudiced** against blacks and who did not respect their hard-working **foreman**.

George McJunkin on his horse, Headless. *What would cowboys do in their jobs?*

prejudice
foreman

Travel and Communication

When New Mexico became part of the United States, there were few roads. There was the old Camino Real to El Paso. And, of course, the Santa Fe Trail was the main road

A stagecoach with a full load of passengers pulls into Silver City. *What would have been some difficulties of stage travel?*

telegraph

to Missouri. Smaller roads and trails joined towns in the territory. All were dusty, with deep ruts and no bridges.

By the 1850s, the government gave money to improve these roads and build new ones. Stagecoaches were beginning to carry passengers and mail across the territory. The stagecoaches needed good roads.

The first stagecoaches traveled the Santa Fe Trail. They left Independence, Missouri, once a month. Another stage line was run by the Butterfield Overland Mail Company. Its coaches traveled between St. Louis and San Francisco. On the way, they passed through southern New Mexico. The

"Butterfield Trail" from end to end was 2,700 miles long. The company stopped service in 1861 when the Civil War began.

The telephone was invented in the mid-1870s. Before that, the **telegraph** was the best way to send messages. The U.S. Army built the first telegraph line to New Mexico. It reached Santa Fe on July 8, 1869. That was a major event in the history of the territory. The telegraph did not reach Mesilla in the south until 1875.

Life on the Santa Fe Trail

Marian Sloan was just eight years old when she first came to New Mexico. The year was 1852. Marian traveled with her mother and her older brother Will. They all rode in a wagon with a caravan on the Santa Fe Trail.

This photo of Marian Sloan Russell and her husband, Lieutenant Richard Russell, was taken about the time they were married in 1865. *What hardships did the wife of an army officer face in the Southwest?*

Years later, Marian Sloan told what it was like. Great herds of buffalo drifted by. Deer and antelope ran past the wagons. Terrible rainstorms came up suddenly. Thunder boomed and lightning flashed. But the storms passed quickly and sunlight brightened the plains.

"It was on this trip," says Marian, "that I first saw a tarantula. It was a big hairy spider. They lived in holes in the ground. When we found a hole, we would stomp on the ground. We would say:

Tarantula, Tarantula!

Come out. Come out!

Tell us what it is all about!

And sure enough, they would come out, walking on long legs. As a reward for having obeyed, we would kill them."

After two months, the caravan reached Santa Fe. There Marian and her family settled down. She and Will attended school. As Marian walked home from school one day, she met Kit Carson. A friendship began that day. The girl saw Kit many times in later years. He always called her "Maid Marian."

In 1864, Marian Sloan was a young woman. Going over the Santa Fe Trail again, she stopped at Fort Union. She met a young army officer there named Richard Russell. Soon they were married.

The host of the dance met us at the door. He led the territorial governor and myself to our seats at the head of the room.

The customs at these dances are very different from those back East. During this season of Lent, people at dances provide themselves with egg-shells filled with perfume water. They break the egg-shells over the heads of friends as a matter of fun.

Three pretty girls came toward the place where the governor and I were sitting. Their faces beamed with mischief. Before we had time to stand, smash! dash! went the egg-shells over our heads. Down our faces streamed the perfume water. The happy girls marched away and took their seats.

—W.W.H. Davis, El Gringo (1856)
(Note: The custom of breaking egg shells at dances is still observed in parts of New Mexico.)

Many years later, Marian Sloan Russell wrote a book called *Land of Enchantment*. She described life in the New Mexico Territory. She told of her adventures on the Santa Fe Trail.

"The magic that old trail held for us!" Marian said. "Seems that folks who made those trips in covered wagons never forgot them."

Wagons on the trail into Santa Fe.

With the coming of the railroad, stagecoaches soon disappeared. *What improvements did train transportation provide?*

But as Marian grew up, the day of the Santa Fe Trail was coming to an end. New Mexicans were dreaming of a railroad. They wanted trains, not wagons and stagecoaches.

Railroads Arrive

New railroads did more than anything else to change life in the territory. The first to enter New Mexico was the Santa Fe Railroad. It followed the old Santa Fe Trail much of the way. In 1878, tracks were laid high over Raton Pass. A train tunnel 613 meters (2,011 feet) long was cut through the top of the pass.

Work crews pushed the tracks forward.

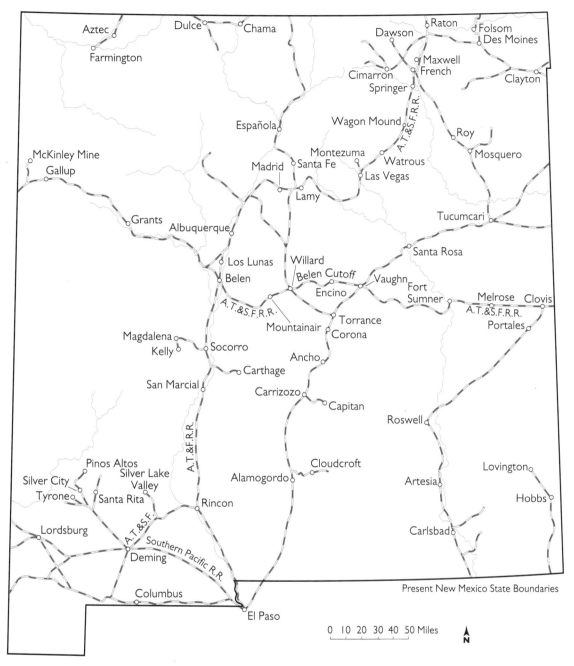

New Mexico's Railroads in 1900

Aztec
Dulce
Chama
Raton
Folsom
Des Moines
Farmington
Dawson
Maxwell
French
Cimarron
Clayton
Springer
Española
Wagon Mound
Roy
A.T.&S.F.R.R.
McKinley Mine
Montezuma
Watrous
Mosquero
Gallup
Madrid
Santa Fe
Las Vegas
Lamy
Grants
Tucumcari
Albuquerque
Santa Rosa
Los Lunas
Willard
Belen
Belen Cutoff
Vaughn
Fort
Encino
Sumner
Melrose
Clovis
A.T.&S.F.R.R.
A.T.&S.F.R.R.
Torrance
Portales
Mountainair
Corona
Magdalena
Socorro
Kelly
Ancho
Carthage
San Marcial
Carrizozo
Capitan
Roswell
A.T.&F.R.R.
Pinos Altos
Cloudcroft
Lovington
Silver Lake
Silver City
Valley
Alamogordo
Artesia
Tyrone
Santa Rita
Hobbs
Lordsburg
Rincon
A.T.&S.F.
Carlsbad
Southern Pacific R.R.
Deming
Present New Mexico State Boundaries
Columbus
El Paso
0 10 20 30 40 50 Miles
N

On July 4, 1879, they reached Las Vegas. Citizens there cheered! They knew trains from the East would bring progress.

Track building continued. The main line passed 18 miles south of Santa Fe, where it turned toward Albuquerque. However, another track was built from Lamy, on the main line, to New Mexico's capital. The people of Santa Fe saw the first engine come puffing into town on February 9, 1880.

By April 5, the Santa Fe Railroad reached Albuquerque. From there it went south. Above Las Cruces, the tracks forked. The east fork went to El Paso. The west fork headed to Deming. At Deming, it met the tracks of the Southern Pacific Railroad, which had been built from California. Now the territory was joined by rails to both the East and West Coasts.

In a short time, other railroads spread a web of track across New Mexico. The Denver and Rio Grande Railroad was one of the most important. It was based in Colorado. This railroad served towns in northern parts of New Mexico.

Effects of the Railroads

The beginning of train service changed New Mexico forever. New people arrived by the thousands. Among the newcomers were many Blacks who worked for the railroad. They were porters and cooks on the trains. Beginning in the 1880s, they and their families introduced Black culture to New Mexico towns, including their food, music, and folklore.

Goods could now be shipped cheaply from the East by rail. Also, farmers and ranchers in the territory could easily ship wool, hides, and farm products. They could even send live cattle and sheep to stockyards in Kansas City and Chicago.

New towns appeared along the railroad lines. And the old towns, dating from Spanish and Mexican days, saw major changes. In Las Vegas, the Santa Fe Railroad bypassed the old town plaza. It built a station a mile to the east. There, East Las Vegas grew up. It became mainly an Anglo town. The frame and brick houses looked like those in New York or Ohio.

The same thing happened in Albuquerque. The Santa Fe tracks and station were placed two miles east of the Old Town Plaza. Soon, new Albuquerque was a rich and growing city. Old Albuquerque became less and less important. There were two Albuquerques, Old and New, until 1949. At that time, they finally joined to become one city. Growth continued. Albuquerque now has more than 600,000 people.

Archbishop John B. Lamy.

A priest teaching
in the open air.

Schools: Their Slow Progress

Schools came late to New Mexico. In
Spanish days, children were taught at home.
Or sometimes a priest gave classes for a few
boys. Padre Antonio José Martínez of Taos,
for example, was a teacher and printer of
school books.

After the Americans arrived, people
decided it was time to have a real school system. But many years would pass before there
were schools for all.

The first schools were started by churches.
The Baptists began a small school at Santa Fe
in 1849. The Methodists started another in
1850. But for a long time, the largest schools

were run by the Catholic Church.

In 1851, John B. Lamy arrived in the territory. He was the first Catholic bishop of New Mexico. He made many changes. He brought in new priests and nuns, and he started many schools. In 1875, Lamy became archbishop. He was one of the famous men of the territorial period.

Only children in the larger towns got to go to the church schools. There were no teachers for the smaller places and Indian *pueblos*. For example, the Indian agent visited Acoma Pueblo in 1870. He found 154 children without a school. Only one person in the village could read and write. The agent said the Indian people wanted an education for their children.

Later, the Albuquerque Indian School was established. It was a boarding school run by the government. Indian children lived there and went to classes. But schools near the homes of Pueblos, Navajos, and Apaches were not built until the twentieth century.

After the railroads came, New Mexicans worked to set up a modern education system. Finally, in 1891, a public school system was started. Amado Chaves (the son of Manuel Chaves) was the first territorial superintendent of education. Church schools continued. But now there were to be free, public schools for all who wanted to attend.

boarding school
superintendent

Sheriff Pat Garrett helped bring law and order to Lincoln County.

Elfego Baca as a young deputy sheriff. *Do you know of any other Hispanic heroes from this period in New Mexico?*

Even before this happened, in 1889 the territorial government had started colleges and universities. These included the University of New Mexico, New Mexico A.&.M. College (today New Mexico State University), and a School of Mines at Socorro. Slowly, New Mexicans were getting the schools they needed.

Outlaws and Lawmen

Schools and railroads were signs of progress. But still New Mexico remained part of the Wild West. Most people wanted a peaceful life. They wanted safety for their children. Yet, a few people were wild and violent. They were the outlaws.

Clay Allison was one of these. From 1875

to 1878, he hung around Cimarron in Colfax County. He killed several men in gunfights. People lived in fear until he left the territory.

Billy the Kid was the best-known of all outlaws. He was a thief and a killer. He killed at least nine men—and perhaps as many as 21. As a boy, he lived in Silver City. He got in trouble there, so he went to Lincoln County in 1877. Lincoln County then covered most of southeastern New Mexico. It was the largest county in the United States.

Many outlaws had come to that part of the territory. Fighting broke out and six-guns blazed. Right in the middle was Billy the Kid. A series of violent events became known as the Lincoln County War.

Finally, in 1878 Lew Wallace was named governor of the territory. Soon, he was able to bring law and order to Lincoln County. The governor had the help of Sheriff Pat Garrett. The sheriff tracked Billy the Kid to Fort Sumner. On the night of July 14, 1881, Garrett shot Billy to death. The young outlaw's life came to an end at age 21.

Other lawmen, like Pat Garrett, helped control violence in the territory. Nineteen-year-old Elfego Baca was a deputy sheriff in 1884. Several dozen Texas cowboys began shooting up the town of Frisco in Socorro County. Baca decided to put a stop to that.

William Bonney, alias Billy the Kid. *Why has he remained a popular figure to this day?*

The cowboys surrounded Elfego Baca in a log hut. For 36 hours, they blazed away at him. Elfego shot back. At least 4,000 bullets struck the hut. However, Elfego Baca escaped unhurt. He became a hero, known all over New Mexico.

The Military

Another group that helped keep peace were soldiers. The army built forts throughout New Mexico to protect settlers. One of the most famous of the army troops were the Buffalo Soldiers of the Ninth and Tenth Cavalry.

The Indians gave them this name because the Black soldiers' curly hair looked like that of the buffalo. It was a name given out of great respect.

The Buffalo Soldiers patrolled eastern New Mexico in the 1870s and early 1880s. They helped open that part of the state to settlers. When the railroad came, the Buffalo Soldiers moved into southern New Mexico. There in the 1880s they helped bring an end to raids by the Apache.

The Buffalo Soldiers were noted for their courage and loyalty. Among them were 11 Medal of Honor winners. When they finished their time in the army, some of the Buffalo Soldiers stayed in New Mexico and became cowboys and others settled in towns.

Becoming a Different Place

Between 1850 and 1900, New Mexico developed rapidly. The rough frontier began to settle down. The Indian Wars passed into history and outlaws slowly disappeared. By the end of the century, the territory was more peaceful. New Mexico was ready to find its place in the modern world.

Words to Know

Americanized   ghost town   rural

boarding school   lumbering   superintendent

foreman   prejudice   telegraph

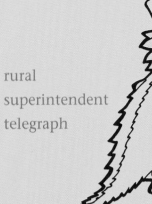

Reviewing What You Have Read

1. Name three New Mexico towns that started as farming and ranching centers.
2. Why did some towns, like Mogollon, become ghost towns?
3. Who was John Chisum?
4. Who was George McJunkin?
5. Why was the telegraph important to New Mexico in the 1870s?
6. Who wrote a book about life in New Mexico called *Land of Enchantment*?
7. What happened in Santa Fe on February 9, 1880?
8. In what year were free, public schools begun in New Mexico?
9. Who was Billy the Kid?
10. Why did Elfego Baca become famous?

For Thought and Discussion

1. How did the railroads help New Mexico to grow?

2. How do you think schools helped New Mexico? Do you think that schools are more important today than they were 100 years ago? Why or why not?

3. Suppose Billy the Kid had lived today. Do you think he would have become famous as an outlaw, or would he be seen as just another criminal?

When bicycles became popular around the turn of
the century, people rode to work on two wheels.
*Do you see any advantages of the bicycle over the
horse or the mule?*

9

A NEW ERA BEGINS

After 1900 life in New Mexico began to move faster. The automobile replaced the horse and wagon. Towns grew into cities. There were good economic times—and bad ones, too. New Mexicans were also asked to support their country in two world wars. As years passed, the state became much more important to the rest of the nation. It helped lead the country into the Atomic Age.

In our story of New Mexico, we have now reached the twentieth century. We have studied exciting events from the past. We have learned about interesting people. Events and people shaped the development of New Mexico.

Scene in front of Albuquerque's First National Bank, about 1905. *How would a photo of this location be different today?*

newcomer

Between 1900 and 1945, things happening elsewhere in the United States began to have more influence on the Southwest. Congress finally let New Mexico become a state. The nation fought in World War I and World War II. And a difficult economic time, known as the depression, brought hardship to many Americans.

Opening of the Twentieth Century

By 1900, New Mexico had nearly 200,000 people. Many were **newcomers**. They had moved here in the 20 years after the railroad arrived. Most of the people lived in the Rio Grande and Pecos valleys. The rest of the territory had plenty of wide open spaces.

Albuquerque was booming. It had become a railroad center. Hundreds of people worked at the railroad shops downtown. Other people worked in businesses and factories. Some went to their jobs on streetcars pulled by mules. Others traveled to work on bicycles. Ranchers and farmers came to Albuquerque to buy and sell.

Other towns were growing, too. Santa Fe,

An Albuquerque
streetcar in 1881.

Las Vegas, Roswell, and Las Cruces offered jobs
to people from rural areas. Many people
moved there to work and live.

Statehood at Last

But New Mexico was still not developing as
fast as it could. That was because, like Arizona,
New Mexico remained a territory. In 1906,
members of Congress wanted New Mexico and
Arizona to be joined together. They would become a single, new state. But that plan was defeated.

An American soldier stands guard over the ruins of Columbus after Pancho Villa's raid.

Then, in 1910, Congress passed an Enabling Act. That act allowed New Mexico to become a state. First, however, a state **constitution** would have to be drawn up. Also, new state officials would have to be elected.

The constitution was ready by August 1911. Soon afterward, an election was held. William C. McDonald was elected the first governor of the state. He was a rancher from Carrizozo. Then, on January 6, 1912, New Mexico became a state. It was the 47th state in the United States.

McDonald took office as governor on January 15, 1912. Special ceremonies were held in Santa Fe. With that, the territory of New Mexico passed into history. As a state, New Mexico looked toward the future with hope.

constitution

The Columbus Raid

During New Mexico's early years as a state, there was trouble on the border. In 1910, a long revolution began in the Republic of Mexico. For years, different groups fought for control of the government.

One Mexican leader in the north of Mexico was Pancho Villa. In March 1916, Villa's men crossed the border into New Mexico. They attacked the town of Columbus, south of Deming. Why Pancho Villa did this is still a mystery.

In this attack, Columbus citizens and American soldiers guarding the town were killed. Many buildings were burned to the ground. Afterward, Villa's men fled across the border and disappeared.

World War I

Soon, New Mexicans had other problems to worry about. In April 1917, the United States entered World War I in Europe. The United States sided with the Allied Powers (England, France, Russia) against the Central Powers (Germany, Austria, Hungary).

New Mexico's National Guard was ordered to fight in the war. The National Guard was made up of citizen soldiers. Camp Funston was set up at the University of New Mexico. It was a training camp for the National Guard.

revolution
National Guard

Most of the young men at the university joined the Guard. All members of the football team joined. Many other New Mexican men also joined. Women had to take on jobs that the men had done. For example, they drove the new electric streetcars that now ran between the university and downtown Albuquerque. Women did many other jobs, too. They worked hard to help our nation win the war.

Men rushed to serve their country from all parts of New Mexico. New Mexico had among the highest number of volunteers of any state. Many of them fought bravely in Europe.

Captain Joseph Quesenberry of Las Cruces was one of the New Mexicans who gave his life in battle. He was the first U.S. Army captain to die in the war. Also, a hundred Navajos, Apaches, and Pueblos served their nation.

In November 1918, World War I came to an end. The Central Powers had been defeated. Across New Mexico, people celebrated. They were happy that the bloody war in Europe was over.

The Flu Disaster

A few weeks before the war was over, a terrible flu epidemic struck New Mexico. An epidemic is a great wave of sickness. The flu, or influenza, spread around the world. Millions

epidemic
influenza

of people died. It was one of the worst epidemics in history.

The first flu cases in the state were recorded in Carlsbad on October 8, 1918. The flu germs were brought by members of a circus from the East. The flu spread rapidly across the state. People wore white masks over their mouths and noses to protect themselves. But the masks did little good.

Some New Mexico towns suffered more from the flu than others. Gallup, Belen, and Socorro had the most victims. But no place was safe. Stores, offices, schools, and universities closed. Many families in New Mexico lost a member or friend to the disease. In all, 5,000 people died of flu in the state.

Epidemics were common in New Mexico's history. The Spaniards first brought diseases like measles and smallpox. In 1780, hundreds of Spanish and Pueblo people died from a terrible smallpox epidemic.

Early health seekers enjoy a sunny porch in Silver City. *Why is New Mexico's climate healthy?*

smallpox

A New Direction in Health Care

The flu epidemic of 1918 showed the need for better health care. In the years before the flu epidemic, a few smallpox cases had been recorded. The state government became concerned about health. As a result, it established a Department of Health in 1919. The department's chief job was to control epidemics. It also hoped to make New Mexico "the healthiest state in the nation."

In fact, New Mexico was already known as a healthy place to live. Its fine climate and clean air were good for people with lung diseases. One of the worst lung diseases was tuberculosis. Then, it was the main cause of death in the United States.

tuberculosis

Thousands of persons with tuberculosis came to New Mexico. They hoped the climate would cure them. Special hospitals were built for them in Santa Fe, Albuquerque, and other towns. Many who got well later became important citizens in the state.

People with bone diseases visited New Mexico's many hot springs. Bathing in the hot waters made them feel better. There were famous hot springs near Las Vegas, Deming, and Truth or Consequences.

The sick who came to New Mexico were called "health-seekers." The health-seekers brought money and new skills to New Mexico. They played an important part in the state's economy. The doctors and hospitals that cared for the health-seekers served other New Mexicans, too. The state continues to offer very good health care today.

This New Mexico family is taking a Sunday drive in a new automobile over 70 years ago. *What do you think it felt like to ride in this car?*

Tourists

Tourists also helped New Mexico's economy. The Santa Fe Railroad worked hard to get people from the East to visit the Southwest. It built fine hotels and set up tours. Visitors were eager to see New Mexico's sights. They came to see the historic buildings and Indian *pueblos*. The Indian people began to make better crafts.

economy

A welcome sign on old U.S. 66, at the New Mexico border west of Gallup. *What Interstate Highway in New Mexico follows much of the old Route 66?*

tourists

Rugs, jewelry, and pottery could be sold to the tourists.

As automobiles became more common, more tourists came. The first car entered New Mexico in 1897. It was driven over Raton Pass from Colorado. By 1910, Albuquerque had only 32 cars. Most people still rode horses or drove wagons. But all that had changed by 1920.

As the Automobile Age dawned, more and more tourists discovered New Mexico. Cars and buses met them at the railroad stations. The tourists were shown the many wonders of the state. In a short time, tourists had become a major part of the state's economy. Route 66 carried cars across the state for decades. Eventually, Interstate 40 replaced Route 66 as the main road across New Mexico.

Workings of the Economy

In earlier chapters we have talked about the economy. The economy has to do with making a living. Money, business, and jobs are all part of the economy.

To make money, businesses offer goods and services that people need or want. When this happens, jobs are created. People with jobs have money to spend. Their spending helps businesses grow and hire more people.

When the economy is good, people put their extra money in banks, as savings. In return, they get a small payment from the bank called interest. The banks then lend money to other people or businesses. With a bank loan, a company can build a new factory. Or a family can build a new house. Saving and lending money keep the economy growing.

Workers often decide to join together and form a labor union. A labor union tries to get more pay or better treatment for workers. If the company says no, the workers may strike. This means that all work stops. A strike causes problems for the economy.

More problems are caused if people lose trust in the economy. When that happens, people begin to take their savings out of the banks. Without the savings, banks cannot lend money to businesses. Then, no new jobs are created, and old jobs may be lost.

Mayor Clyde Tingley (right), poses with a famous pilot, Charles Lindbergh, 1929.

interest
labor union

Young and old New Mexico farmers pose with their prize pigs during the Great Depression.

When there are problems with the economy, businesses fail. Money becomes hard to get. More and more workers lose their jobs. Finally, some banks fail. They no longer have enough money to pay back all the savings of citizens. This results in what we call an economic depression.

America's Great Depression

Most large businesses are owned by many individuals. Each person buys a part of the business. Each person gets stocks. These are papers showing the amount the stockholder owns. Stocks are always being bought and sold. The places where this is done are called stock exchanges.

On October 24, 1929, prices on the New York Stock Exchange crashed. That is, the price of stocks suddenly fell very low. Everyone wanted to sell stocks but no one wanted to buy. Americans had lost trust in their economy.

The stock market crash was the start of the Great Depression. It was the worst economic time in the history of the United

States. Factories went out of business. Farmers lost their land. Jobs disappeared, and banks closed. The depression spread across the nation.

New Mexico, too, was caught in the Great Depression. The hard times lasted through the 1930s. Many banks failed and people lost their life's savings. Some counties could not provide enough money to run schools. Teachers could not be paid, so schools closed. Not many tourists visited the state. Few families could afford vacations any longer.

The Slow Recovery

The government in Washington tried to help the people. It gave money to create public jobs. In New Mexico, this money was used for building projects around the state. Many New Mexicans got jobs under this program.

In 1934, Clyde Tingley became governor of New Mexico. He was a friend of President Franklin Roosevelt. Governor Tingley made many trips to Washington, D.C. He worked hard to get more government money for the state. As a result, things slowly got better in New Mexico.

Something else helped New Mexico—the oil business. In 1899, companies had begun looking for oil near Farmington. By 1913, wells were pumping oil in the San Juan Basin in northwest New Mexico. This business boosted

A farm during the Dust Bowl of the 1930s. *How can you tell sand has been blown around?*

boom town

the state's economy. Farmington, Aztec, and Bloomfield became famous names in the oil business.

Oil was also found in the southeast part of the state. Some of the first wells were near Artesia. Later, a lot more oil was discovered near Lovington, Eunice, Jal, and Hobbs. They became oil **boom towns**. Workers filled their streets. Small businesses grew rich. Oil helped New Mexicans get through the Great Depression.

The Dust Bowl

People in Union County around Clayton had another problem. For three years in the 1930s, almost no rain fell in that area. There, and in neighboring states, the ground became dry as powder. Strong winds caused dust storms that turned the sky black. Soil on farms and ranches was blown away.

This area became known as the Dust Bowl. Farmers could not grow crops. Family after family gave up and headed for California. In old cars, they crossed New Mexico. They were another sign of hardship during the depression years.

New Mexico's Economy in 1940

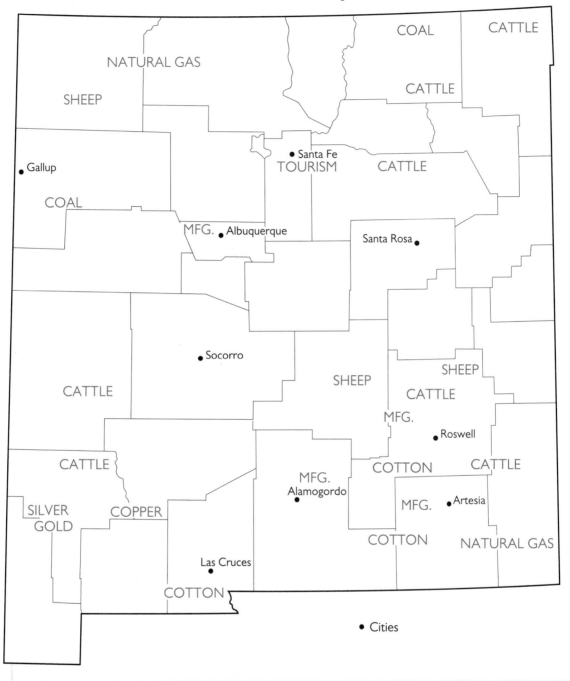

New Mexican soldiers trained for World War II at Camp Luna, near Las Vegas. *Can you tell from this soldier's uniform where he will be sent to fight?*

Many New Mexico Indians, like this Navajo, served in the military during World War II. *Do you have relatives who served in the armed forces during World War II?*

One unit of the New Mexico National Guard that surrendered at Bataan was the 200th Coast Artillery. After the war, General Nathan Wainwright praised the brave New Mexicans in this unit. He said:

> *The 200th Coast Artillery was the first unit in the Philippines to go into action and fire at the enemy. It was also the first to go into action defending our flag in the Pacific and the last to lay down its arms.*

World War II

Americans had hoped that World War I would be the last great war. But that was not to be. On December 7, 1941, Japan attacked Pearl Harbor in Hawaii. The United States entered its second great war. For the next four years, our nation fought against Japan, Germany, and Italy.

New Mexico played an important part in World War II. Once again, the state's National Guard went off to fight. Part of the Guard was sent to defend the Philippine Islands.

Early in the war, Japan conquered the Philippines. About 1,800 New Mexicans were captured. With other Americans, they were forced to walk 65 miles through the jungle. Many died or were killed. This walk was the terrible Bataan Death March. It became a sad part of New Mexico's history.

The war ended the depression. All at once, there were jobs for everyone. Workers were needed on farms and in factories. Men and women were needed in the armed forces. War made the nation's economy grow again.

In New Mexico, Indians, Hispanos, blacks, and Anglos eagerly joined to defend their country. A group of Navajos from New Mexico and Arizona played a special part. They were Marines who became the famous "code talkers."

These Navajos helped in the war against Japan. They helped their nation conquer islands in the Pacific Ocean held by Japan. They sent messages by radio. The Navajos spoke in their own language and used a code. The Japanese heard the radio messages. But they could not understand the Navajo code. By war's end, 400 Indian code talkers were serving in the U.S. Marines. At the battle of Iwo Jima they had sent hundreds of messages, contributing to the victory. A Japanese officer said later: "We could never break the code because we did not understand the Navajo language." Today, an exhibit on the code talkers can be seen at the Pentagon in Washington, D.C.

The Atomic Bomb

Early in the war, the U.S. government decided to build an atomic bomb. The government hoped such a bomb would end the war quickly and save American lives.

Work on the first atomic bomb began in 1942. The work was done at a little-known place in New Mexico. The place was the Los Alamos Ranch School west of Santa Fe. Scientists worked there in secret.

Scientists came from all parts of the world to work at Los Alamos. Dr. J. Robert Oppenheimer was in charge of the work.

No one had ever built an atomic bomb. So work on the bomb took a lot of time.

code
atomic bomb

The world's first atomic bomb exploded on the desert of central New Mexico in July 1945. *How did the atomic bomb change the world?*

At first, from the darkness, came the light: a stupendous [awesome] burst of fierce light many times more brilliant than the sun. Instantly the surrounding desert and mountains were bathed in white brilliance. Even those with their eyes closed were able to sense the explosion of light and feel the warmth of it on their bodies. Almost everyone was momentarily blinded and dazed. Those recovering first turned to see through their welder's glasses a huge ball of fire, like the sun, rising from the desert floor in a swirling inferno of reds and oranges and yellows.

—A description of the first atomic bomb explosion, as seen by scientists from two miles away. From *City of Fire*, by James W. Kunetka

On August 6, 1945, the *Santa Fe New Mexican* ran a headline, "Los Alamos Secret." In the story, New Mexicans first read of the existence of the city of Los Alamos, then two years old:

Santa Fe learned officially today of a city of 6,000 in its own front yard. Decision to locate the Atomic Bomb Project Laboratory on a mesa an hour's drive from Santa Fe meant that it was necessary for the Army Engineers to construct an entirely new town to house the workers and their families. Primary reason for selection of the isolated site was security.

Twice a year Trinity Site is opened to visitors.

Everything was done in secret. From 1943 to 1945, New Mexicans had no idea what was happening in Los Alamos.

By early summer, 1945, the bomb was ready for testing. It was taken south to a place in the desert between Socorro and Alamogordo. There Apaches had once hunted. And Spaniards had passed nearby on El Camino Real. Dr. Oppenheimer named the testing place the Trinity Site.

Early on the morning of July 16, 1945, the world's first atomic bomb was exploded. A bright light flashed across the sky. In Albuquerque, people were shaken from their beds by the blast. Windows were broken as far away as Gallup.

The government still wanted to keep the bomb a secret. It said an army ammunition dump had blown up. The truth was not known until the following month. In August, atomic bombs made in Los Alamos were dropped on the Japanese cities of Hiroshima and Nagasaki. Only then did the world learn what scientists had been doing in New Mexico.

The Atomic Age

The atomic bomb finally ended World War II. But the end of the war did not mean the end of work at Los Alamos Scientific Laboratory. Soon there were new jobs to do. Scientists worked on new kinds of atomic weapons. More importantly, they explored peaceful uses of atomic energy.

Events at Los Alamos during the war set New Mexico in a new direction. Until then, the state had been best known for its beautiful land and history. But now people everywhere thought of New Mexico in another way. They thought of it as a place of scientific work. They expected New Mexico to help point the way toward the future.

Aerial view of Los Alamos Scientific Laboratory. *Why did the national government choose this site for the location of its atomic laboratories?*

Words to Know

atomic bomb   economy   labor union   smallpox

boom town   epidemic   National Guard   stocks

code   influenza   newcomer   tourist

constitution   interest   revolution   tuberculosis

depression

Reviewing What You Have Read

1. In what year did New Mexico become a state?
2. Who was the first governor of the state?
3. What town in New Mexico did Pancho Villa attack in 1916?
4. Why did many people with lung diseases move to New Mexico in the 1920s?
5. What was the worst economic time in the history of the United States called?
6. Why did such towns as Lovington and Hobbs become boom towns during the 1930s?
7. In the Southwest, what was the Dust Bowl?
8. How did World War II help end the Great Depression?
9. How did Navajo "code talkers" help win the war in the Pacific?
10. Where in New Mexico was the first atomic bomb developed?

For Thought and Discussion

1. How did women in New Mexico gain new opportunities for work during World War I?

2. How did the automobile help to make tourism an important business in New Mexico? How important is this business today? Tell how tourism brings money to people in our state.

3. Why do you think that the atomic bomb was developed in New Mexico?

Irrigation is necessary to grow crops in New Mexico. This field is located in the Mesilla Valley near Las Cruces. *What would happen to New Mexico's rivers and streams if there were no restrictions on irrigation?*

10

MODERN NEW MEXICO

New Mexico has its share of social and economic problems. Prejudice is one of these problems. There are not enough good jobs for everyone. We have not yet learned how to conquer many diseases. And we also need to solve our future energy needs. History cannot give us the answers to these problems. But it can show us how to look for them.

Our story of New Mexico has taken us through many centuries. Together, we have traveled the long road from the past. By now, we can see that history has made New Mexico what it is today.

In 1998 over 1,650,000 people lived in our state. Half the people lived in the eleven largest cities: Albuquerque, Las Cruces, Santa Fe, Roswell, Clovis, Farmington, Hobbs, Carlsbad, Gallup, Rio Rancho, and Las Vegas. The rest lived in small towns and in the country.

New Mexicans today have many different ways of life. Most Indian people live on reservations. They continue to follow many of the old ways of Indian life. Other Indians choose to live in cities. Indians contribute in important ways to New Mexico's social, political, and economic life.

In the northern mountains, many Hispanos prefer living in quiet rural areas. But others have moved to the cities in recent years. There they have found new opportunities. Many Hispanos are leaders in law, government, business, and education.

Anglos were newcomers to the state. They had to adjust to life in New Mexico. The task of adjusting is still going on. Life here is not like life in the East. Water is scarce here. Many everyday customs appear strange. Attitudes are different. These things have changed the way of life of Anglos in New Mexico. The Anglo, the Indian, the Hispano, and the black have had a part in making New Mexico what it is today.

During the last thirty years, other groups of people from foreign lands have made New Mexico their home. The largest number of foreign-born are from Mexico and Central

America. But some people have come from Europe, too: from England, France, Germany, Spain, Italy, and Poland. Asian countries like Korea, Vietnam, Japan, India, and Pakistan have also contributed new citizens to New Mexico. Each group has added something different to our state.

In this chapter, we will look at some of the problems New Mexicans have faced in recent years. We will see how the people in the state are learning to deal with the modern world.

María Martínez smooths the surface of a pot. *Where do you see pots like these today?*

Indians in the New Age

Until World War II, Indian communities in New Mexico were very isolated. Dirt roads led to most reservations. Many Indians still drove wagons to town or to trading posts. Indians living on reservations were not allowed to vote until 1948.

New Mexico's Indians lived apart from American society. They did not have the same benefits as other citizens. But after the war, things began to change.

isolated

Native American Reservations and Pueblos Today

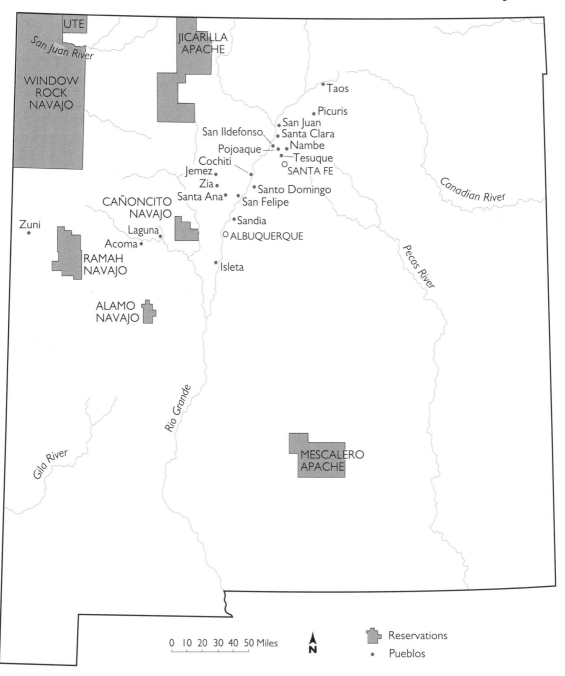

UTE

JICARILLA APACHE

San Juan River

WINDOW ROCK NAVAJO

Taos

Picuris

San Juan

San Ildefonso
Santa Clara
Pojoaque
Nambe
Cochiti
Tesuque
Jemez
SANTA FE
Zia
Santa Ana
Santo Domingo
San Felipe

Canadian River

CAÑONCITO NAVAJO

Zuni

Sandia
ALBUQUERQUE
Laguna

Acoma

RAMAH NAVAJO

Isleta

Pecos River

ALAMO NAVAJO

Rio Grande

Gila River

MESCALERO APACHE

0 10 20 30 40 50 Miles

N

Reservations

• Pueblos

Many young Indian men served with honor during World War II. They traveled to other parts of the United States. They fought in Europe and Asia. The young men saw new things and developed new ideas.

When they returned home, Indian soldiers wanted to improve their communities. They hoped for better schools, jobs, and health care. But sometimes older Indians worried. They feared that change might come too fast. Such change might destroy the heart of Indian culture. Old customs, they believed, should be kept.

The conflict between the new and the old caused stress among some Indian groups. The stresses grew as change speeded up in the 1960s and 1970s. Indian people tried hard to hold onto their old ways. At the same time, they tried to adjust to the fast-changing world around them.

Professor Alfonso Ortiz has taught Indian culture at Princeton University in New Jersey and at the University of New Mexico.

The Pueblos

New Mexico has 19 Pueblo groups. The only other Pueblos are the Hopis. This group lives in Arizona. Farming has become less important in recent years. Today, many Pueblos work in towns. Many living close to Los Alamos find work at the scientific laboratory.

Lately, the demand for Pueblo crafts has

crafts

Young people at Jemez Indian Pueblo race during a celebration.

grown. Many people can make a living at home. They have become fine artists. Their paintings, pottery, and jewelry bring high prices. Fine potters like María Martínez of San Ildefonso and Lucy Lewis of Acoma have become famous.

Pueblo boys and girls take part in village life. They learn old customs and ceremonies from their parents. Some are learning to make Indian crafts. At school, they learn about the world beyond the *pueblo*.

The Pueblos have always been good runners. Jemez, San Juan, and other villages hold long-distance races. Young people like to run. The older people enjoy these races, too.

Beryl Blue Spruce was the first Pueblo Indian medical doctor (M.D.). He received his medical degree in 1964. As a doctor, he worked hard to help Indian people. Dr. Blue Spruce also helped start the American Association of Indian Physicians. In 1957, he told why he wanted to become a doctor:

At present, among the Pueblo tribes of the Southwest, there is not a single Indian doctor, and medical care of the Indian is a function of a separate branch of the Public Health. Although in some regions the work of this organization is noteworthy, in most Indian hospitals and clinics the lack of dedicated personnel is vividly demonstrated by outmoded facilities and a profound disregard for the Indians themselves.

After he became a doctor, Beryl Blue Spruce also said this:

[A doctor] should understand and accept the people he is working with. No one can understand a group of people as well as a member of that group.

More and more Pueblo youths are attending colleges and universities. They are studying to be teachers, lawyers, and doctors. Alfonso Ortiz of San Juan and David Warren of Santa Clara have each earned several university degrees. They are very fine teachers. Both serve as examples for Pueblo young people.

Blue Lake

melting pot

The United States is sometimes said to be a melting pot. Many peoples and cultures have melted or blended together to become Americans. There are strong pressures for everyone to conform—to act and think alike.

The sacred Blue Lake of the Taos Indians. *What is the importance of protecting sites like this one?*

But our country is also a land of freedom. We accept that people should be free to go their own way. We believe that no one should be forced to join the melting pot.

As you can see, there are two forces pulling in different directions. The Pueblos are often caught between these forces. On the one hand, they want to be good Americans. On the other, they do not want to give up all of their Indian ways.

The Blue Lake conflict is a recent example of this problem. Blue Lake is in the mountains above Taos Pueblo. It is a holy place for the Indian people. Religious ceremonies are held there.

In 1906, Blue Lake became part of the Carson National Forest. It was opened to the public. People went there to hunt, fish, and hike. Some of them did not respect the lake. They left trash and cut down trees.

The Taos Indians asked that Blue Lake be given to them. They wanted to protect the lake and the forest around it. But the U.S. government refused. It said that public lands and waters should be open to everyone.

Many non-Indians in New Mexico agreed with the Taos Indians. They believed Indian religion and rights should be protected. In the United States, different cultures should be respected, they said.

The Taos Indians tried to get the land for many years. They went to court many times. Finally, they won. In 1970, Congress gave the *pueblo* 48,000 acres of forest land, including Blue Lake. It was an important victory for Indian rights.

The Navajos

The Navajos are the largest Indian group in the United States. There are now more than 200,000 Navajos, and the number is growing. Most of these people live on a 14 million acre reservation in New Mexico, Arizona, and Utah.

Two other small groups of Navajos live outside the main reservation. The Alamo band has a small reservation north of Magdalena. The Cañoncito Navajos live between Albuquerque and Laguna.

Since 1969, the tribe has called itself the Navajo Nation. The capital, with tribal offices, is at Window Rock. This town is near Gallup, just across the Arizona border. In New Mexico, Gallup and Shiprock are important trade and supply centers for the Navajo people.

A beautiful Two Grey Hills rug woven by Navajos in western New Mexico. *Why are rugs like this one highly prized?*

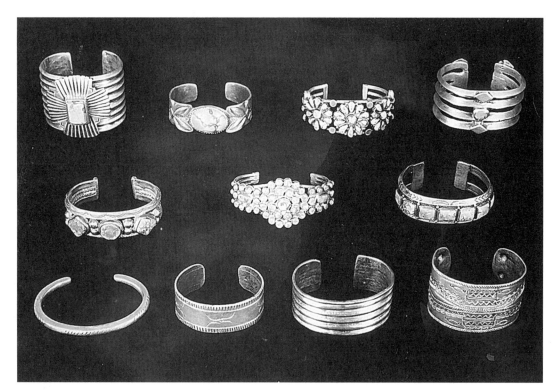

The Indians of New Mexico are famous for their fine silver and turquoise jewelry. *Why did the silver jewelry industry come to New Mexico?*

uranium

Ways of making a living have changed over the years. Many Navajos still farm and raise sheep. But others now have new kinds of jobs on the reservation. Coal, gas, oil and **uranium** are found on Navajo lands. Forests in the Chuska Mountains are cut for lumber. At a sawmill there, a whole new town—Navajo, New Mexico—was recently started. The sawmill offers jobs to tribal members.

Some Navajos earn money by making crafts. The Navajos are famous for their rugs and jewelry. Beautiful hand-woven Navajo rugs bring high prices. Tourists seek out

Navajo silver and turquoise jewelry. The Navajos themselves like to wear it, too. The tribe runs the Navajo Arts and Crafts Guild. The Guild encourages the workers and it helps find a market for their products.

For a long while, most Navajo children could not go to school. They were scattered far apart on the huge reservation. In recent years, things have improved. New schools have been built in isolated areas. Buses carry students over long distances to these schools.

The tribe provides money to help young people attend colleges and universities. The tribe also built its own college on the reservation, called Navajo Community College. It is one of the few colleges on an Indian reservation run by Indian people.

The Navajos have not joined the melting pot. On the reservation, the customs and language are Navajo. Young and old are proud to be what they are. They honor their old ways. But, like the Pueblo people, they are also proud to be Americans.

These Mescalero Apache boys got dressed up in the 1890s to have their picture taken.

The Apaches

The Apache people fought against American rule longer than any other tribe. But once on reservations, they worked hard to learn a new way of life. In New Mexico, theirs is a story of success.

There are about 5,000 Apaches in New Mexico today. About half are Jicarilla. The other half are Mescalero. Their reservations are more than 320 kilometers (200 miles) apart.

The Mescaleros have beautiful mountain lands near Ruidoso. They raise fine cattle. The tribe also earns money by selling lumber and Christmas trees.

Tourism is important, too. Many people visit the reservation to ski in the winter. The Mescaleros borrowed money from the U.S. government and bought a ski resort at Sierra Blanca. They built the Inn of the Mountain Gods on Lake Mescalero. These businesses provide jobs for tribal members, especially young people.

The Jicarillas, far to the north, also make money from tourism and from raising livestock. Their large reservation runs 105 kilometers (65 miles) south from the Colorado border. Tribal offices are at the town of Dulce.

Jicarilla means "little basket." Once, the tribe was famous for making baskets, but only a few are made today. In September, the tribe holds a two-day celebration. They hold races and dances. At this time, the people honor their Apache heritage.

heritage

After World War II, Hispanos began moving away from small farms like this one. *Why did Hispanics move away from their villages? Where did they go?*

Hispanos in the New Age

Like their Indian neighbors, Hispanos have been forced to adjust to a changing world. Until World War II, small villages remained centers of Spanish culture. But with the war, many people left. Some moved to cities like Albuquerque, Santa Fe, and Las Vegas. Others went to California to work in wartime factories. Villages grew smaller. A few became ghost towns.

As New Mexico changed, it became harder for Hispanos to live by farming or ranching. Many of the four million acres in Spanish land grants had been lost. What was left was often too small to support families in today's world.

Jorge López, a famous wood-carver from the mountain village of Córdova. *What kinds of figures does he carve?*

In the 1960s, a small group of Hispanos formed an organization called the Alianza. The group was led by Reies López Tijerina. They hoped to get back the lost land grants. Members asked the governor and the president of the United States to help them. But nothing was done.

The Alianza decided to take the land they felt was theirs. In 1966, group members took over lands in the national forest. The following year, leaders of the Alianza carried out the famous "raid on Tierra Amarilla Courthouse." There was much shooting in the town of Tierra Amarilla. Two lawmen were wounded. Because of the raid, Alianza members went to jail. Trying to get back land grants by force had failed.

The question of land grants is not settled even now. Hispanos and others are still working to solve the problem. They hope some day the U.S. Congress will study the matter. Perhaps then a fair way to solve the problem can be found.

By 1960, more than half of New Mexico's Hispanos had moved to large towns or cities. In moving, they left behind old Spanish ways of life. In the hurry of city life, customs from the past have been lost.

In the last several years, however, young people have become more interested in Spanish culture. Since the 1970s, young artists, writers, and craft workers have developed in the Hispano community. They look to the past for new ideas. Their work can be seen at yearly markets in Santa Fe and Albuquerque.

Hispanic customs and the Hispano people have added much to modern New Mexico. They have helped give life in the state a rare and interesting flavor.

New Mexico Finds Its Place

For many years, people in the East hardly knew that New Mexico was part of the United States. Some even thought it belonged to the Republic of Mexico. But that slowly changed between 1950 and 1990. In those years, New Mexico grew more important to the rest of the country.

In 1950, a Navajo named Paddy Martínez discovered uranium ore near Grants. Uranium is a metal needed in making atomic energy. Grants quickly became a boom town. Some called it "the uranium capital of the world." New Mexico soon was the nation's leading producer of uranium. It held that position until the mid-1980s.

atomic energy

Uranium miners near Grants dug the ore needed in America's nuclear industry.
What is uranium used for?

Since then most uranium mining has stopped.

Meanwhile, atomic research continued at the Los Alamos Scientific Laboratory. The town of Los Alamos had grown to 12,584 people by 1960. Similar research was being done at Albuquerque's Sandia Laboratories. Atomic research and uranium mining made New Mexico famous.

Aerospace Research

New Mexico also became famous for aerospace research and testing. Aerospace has to do with airplanes and spacecraft. During World War II, jet airplanes were invented. Some of these jets were tested in New Mexico. Rockets and guided missiles were also tested here.

In the 1930s, Robert H. Goddard worked in Roswell. He was known as the "father of modern rocketry." His early testing of rockets helped the country send a spacecraft to the moon in 1969.

Holloman Air Force Base at Alamogordo developed an important test program.

research
aerospace
spacecraft

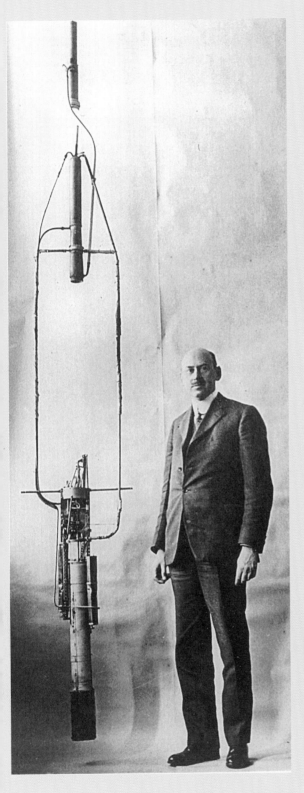

There are now about 6,000 persons working at the Los Alamos Scientific Laboratory, both in research and in support of research. This has made it one of the outstanding science facilities in the nation.

All programs have one common goal—development of new and alternative energy sources and conservation of existing energy supplies.

—From the Los Alamos Laboratory
Report, 1974

Landing of *Columbia* at White Sands.

Dr. Robert Goddard launched a rocket near Roswell on December 30, 1930. *How are rockets used today?*

At the nearby White Sands Missile Range, thousands of guided missiles were fired. As the space program grew, so did the part played by White Sands. In March 1982, thousands of people watched as the first U.S. space shuttle landed there. The International Space Hall of Fame at Alamogordo honors those who have led the way in space.

New Mexico is also the home of one of the largest instruments used in astronomy. Astronomy is the study of the stars and the planets. This instrument is called a VLA (Very Large Array). It is made up of 27 giant dish-shaped antennas spread over 61 kilometers (38 miles).

The VLA was finished in 1980, on the plains west of Magdalena. It receives radio signals from space. The signals help astronomers learn about the sun, planets, and stars.

A Sunbelt State

The southern half of the United States is called the sunbelt. New Mexico is a part of this region. The climate in the sunbelt is good, so many businesses and workers have moved here. Because of this, more and more people now live in the sunbelt. Colder parts of the country have been losing people.

As New Mexico became a sunbelt state, its growth speeded up. New buildings changed

guided missiles
space shuttle
astronomy
antennas
sunbelt

the skylines of cities and towns. Freeways reached out in all directions. Shopping centers drew people to the suburbs. Shopping centers also have sprung up on the Navajo and Jicarilla Apache reservations. As all these newcomers arrive, New Mexico begins to look more and more like other parts of the country.

The Energy Problem

The nation is facing a growing energy problem. Oil and natural gas are being used up. Newer ways to make energy, like atomic power plants, are not always safe. Americans are looking for new ideas to solve the energy problem.

New Mexico produces a lot of natural gas, oil, uranium, and coal. Much of this is sent to other states. These places need the energy that New Mexico produces. But our state cannot produce all the energy that is needed. So we must all look for new ways to make energy.

Solar panels on this university building in Portales make use of the sun's energy for heating. *What are other uses for solar energy?*

A New Mexico style solar house, with greenhouse attached on the right.

Lately, many New Mexicans have become very interested in solar energy. This is energy from the sun. Solar energy can be used to heat homes and public buildings. Many homes across the state now have solar collectors on the roof. These collectors store the sun's energy. This energy is then used for heat.

The wind is another natural form of energy. Wind power can be used to make electricity. It can also be used to turn windmills and pump water. Clayton, in northeastern New Mexico, had a wind turbine. It looked like a giant airplane propeller on top of a steel tower. Wind turned the blades and produced enough electricity for 35 homes.

Right now, wind and solar power supply only a small part of New Mexico's energy needs. Those needs grow year by year. Much research will be needed to prepare us for the future. There is no easy answer to the energy problem.

Looking Ahead

Boys and girls of today will be the men and women of tomorrow. Someday it will be your turn to help make New Mexico a better place. Everyone has something to offer. Each person can help build our future.
Perhaps you are already thinking about the part you can play.

solar energy
turbine

Words to Know

aerospace   crafts   melting pot   space shuttle

antenna   guided missile   research   sunbelt

astronomy   heritage   solar energy   turbine

atomic energy   isolated   spacecraft   uranium

Reviewing What You Have Read

1. How did Indian soldiers who served in World War II help change Indian life when they returned to New Mexico?
2. Why did some Indians not want to see things change?
3. Who is María Martínez?
4. How does the Inn of the Mountain Gods on Lake Mescalero help the Apaches?
5. What did the Alianza try to do by force in the 1960s?
6. Why did Grants become a boom town in the 1950s?
7. What did Robert H. Goddard do in New Mexico in the 1930s?
8. How does the VLA near Magdalena help astronomers ?
9. Why have many Americans moved to New Mexico, a sunbelt state?
10. Name four sources of energy that are produced in New Mexico.

For Thought and Discussion

1. Why do you think Blue Lake was such an important issue to the Pueblo people?

2. How does tourism help our state? In what ways might tourism hurt our state?

3. There are many new sources of energy. These include atomic energy and solar energy. Which forms of energy do you think are best for New Mexico? Why?

Candidates for political office in Chloride have their picture taken in 1910. *What does the number of bars, or stripes, mean on the American flag? What does the number of stars mean?*

11

NEW MEXICO GOVERNMENT

Every citizen should understand how our government works. Each American can play a part in our government. That way, we can all help to keep the government running properly. What part in government will you play? Learning about our government can help you find out.

People must live by rules or laws. Without laws, there would be little order in society. Groups of people everywhere in the world set up governments. A government makes and enforces the laws.

We should all know something about our government and how it works. Citizens take part in government by voting and by telling their views on things. Some citizens become politicians and run for office. Those who are elected become our representatives.

Our form of government is a representative democracy. In a democracy, people govern themselves. Elected representatives speak for the people. These representatives are guided by the United States Constitution. The Constitution is a set of basic laws for our nation. It became our basic law guide in 1789.

Government has different levels. At the top level is the federal (or national) government. The main federal government offices are in Washington, D.C. Then, at another level are the governments of each of the 50 states. Below them are county and city governments.

All these levels of government are closely connected. Each depends upon the others. Together, they form the American system of democracy. In this chapter, we will see how this system works in New Mexico. But first, we should describe Indian and Spanish governments before the Americans came.

Indian Ways of Governing

The Pueblo Indians had their own form of government when the Spaniards arrived in 1540. Each village ruled itself. Each was

politician
democracy
federal

independent. The religious leaders, or *caciques,* were also the government leaders. The *caciques* were the oldest and wisest men in the village.

The Spaniards brought a new form of government to the Pueblos. This was an elected government. Each January, the Indian people elected a governor and other officials. The Spaniards gave the Indian governors black canes. These canes showed that the governors had a right to hold office.

After independence, the Mexican government presented each pueblo with a new cane. Finally, third canes were given to the Indian villages by President Abraham Lincoln in 1863. They were black with silver heads and had Lincoln's name engraved on them. Today, the Spanish, Mexican, and American canes are passed to each governor upon his election. He cares for them during his term.

The Indian governor of San Juan Pueblo poses with his wife and child about 1930. *What symbol of his office does he carry?*

The province of New Mexico is divided into eight districts. Each is run by an alcalde *who serves without pay. The* alcaldes *are under the political and military governor who lives in Santa Fe, the capital. The governor does not even have a clerk, because there is none in the whole province.*

Primary education is given only to children whose parents pay the salary of a teacher. In the capital it has been impossible to find a school teacher and furnish education for everyone. Of course, there are no colleges of any kind.

—Comments on government and education by Pedro Pino, 1812

council
monarchy

The Utes, Apaches, and other tribes were divided into small groups called bands. Each band had a leader. The leader was brave and wise. Tribal laws were not written down. However, everyone knew what the laws were. Since the bands were small, everyone could speak before a tribal council and have a say. This democratic system of government served the Indians well.

The Spanish Empire

Spain and its colonies in other lands were joined together in an empire. This empire was not a democracy. It was a monarchy, ruled by a king. The king, and the people who served in his government, made the laws. They had the last word in everything. Citizens in a monarchy have few rights.

The king of Spain sent a representative to govern in Mexico City. He was the viceroy of New Spain. The viceroy was in charge of the northern frontier. This frontier included New Mexico, Texas, and California. In each of these places, the viceroy named someone to serve as governor.

The governor of the New Mexico colony lived in an adobe "palace" on the plaza in Santa Fe. He had his offices there, too. Spanish soldiers lived behind the palace. The governor also was the military commander of these soldiers.

The governor appointed, or named, other officials to govern in the towns and in the countryside. These officials were known as *alcaldes*. The *alcalde* was mayor and judge. He also measured the land grants that were given to citizens. And he acted to enforce the laws of the king.

Mexico Governs

As we have seen, New Spain broke away from the empire in 1821. The nation of Mexico was begun. In 1824, Mexico became a republic with a constitution. Now citizens

The national emblem of the Republic of Mexico.

alcalde

could elect their *alcaldes*. They could also elect officials to represent them in a national congress.

In many ways, the new government in Mexico was like that of the United States. In other ways, it was not. For example, Mexico had an official church—the Catholic Church. The United States had no official church or religion. People were free to choose their own religion.

As we learned earlier, the United States took over New Mexico in 1846. It was placed under a territorial form of government. New Mexico did not become a state until 1912.

BRANCHES OF GOVERNMENT

Senate House of Representatives	Governor Lieutenant Governor Secretary of State Treasurer Attorney General	State Supreme Court Court of Appeals District Court Magistrate Court
LEGISLATIVE *passes laws*	**EXECUTIVE** *carries out laws*	**JUDICIAL** *decides about laws*

This is the House of Representatives chamber in the State Capitol Building. *Who might use the seats on the second floor?*

The Federal Government

The United States government is divided into three parts, or branches. These are the Congress, the President, and the Supreme Court. They are all in Washington, D.C., our nation's capital.

The **legislative branch**, headed by Congress, passes laws. The **executive branch**, under the president, carries out the laws. The **judicial branch**, which includes the Supreme Court and other courts, decides if laws are proper. The courts also settle arguments, or cases, brought before them.

Having three branches of government protects our democracy. One branch cannot

legislative branch
executive branch
judicial branch

The capital complex at Santa Fe is the nerve center of state government.

tell the other branches what to do. Each branch has some power. That way, there is a balance of power. It is a good system that has lasted more than 200 years.

Under the federal government, the 50 states are tied together. Within limits, each state governs its own affairs. But it also has responsibilities to the country as a whole. New Mexico is just one state. Yet, it plays an important part in making the system of government work.

The State Government

Under our state government is a whole system of local government. The state sets rules for county, city, town, and village government. State government affects our everyday lives in many ways.

The New Mexico Constitution was adopted in 1911. This constitution set up the state government. In Santa Fe, as in Washington, government is divided into three branches. This provides a system of balances at the local level.

The New Mexico legislature makes laws

for the state, much like Congress passes laws for the nation. Our legislature is at the head of the legislative branch. It has two houses, or parts. One house is called the senate. The other is called the house of representatives. Both houses have to agree before a new law can be passed.

The executive branch is the second branch of state government. The governor is the chief executive. The governor carries out the laws passed by the legislature. Other executive officials are a lieutenant governor, secretary of state, treasurer, and an attorney general. The attorney general is the lawyer for the state.

Third is the judicial branch. At its head is the state supreme court. This court hears appeals from lower courts. That is, it makes final decisions. Among the lower courts is the court of appeals, set up by the legislature in 1966. It helps the supreme court. Others are the district courts and the magistrate courts. Magistrate courts serve every city, town, and village. These courts provide justice for all citizens.

The leading officials in each branch of government are elected by the voters. In that way, citizens decide how the government is to be run. The elected officials also appoint others to help them. For example, the executive branch is divided into 13 departments. The head of each department

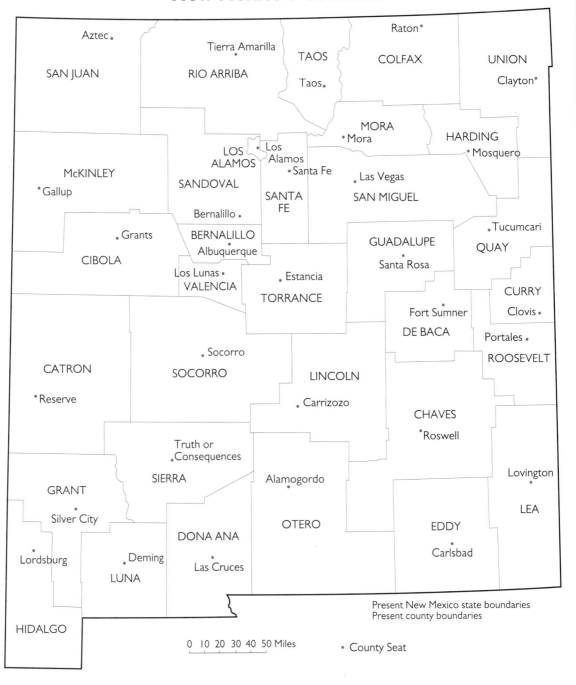

New Mexico's Counties

Aztec •

Tierra Amarilla •

Raton •

TAOS

COLFAX

UNION

Clayton •

SAN JUAN

RIO ARRIBA

Taos •

MORA

Mora •

HARDING

Mosquero •

McKINLEY

Gallup •

LOS ALAMOS

Los Alamos •

SANDOVAL

Santa Fe •

Las Vegas •

SAN MIGUEL

Grants •

Bernalillo •

SANTA FE

Tucumcari •

CIBOLA

BERNALILLO

Albuquerque •

GUADALUPE

Santa Rosa •

QUAY

Los Lunas •

VALENCIA

Estancia •

TORRANCE

CURRY

Clovis •

CATRON

Reserve •

Socorro •

SOCORRO

Fort Sumner •

DE BACA

Portales •

ROOSEVELT

LINCOLN

Carrizozo •

CHAVES

Roswell •

Truth or Consequences •

SIERRA

Alamogordo •

Lovington •

LEA

GRANT

Silver City •

DONA ANA

OTERO

EDDY

Carlsbad •

Lordsburg •

Deming •

LUNA

Las Cruces •

HIDALGO

Present New Mexico state boundaries
Present county boundaries

0 10 20 30 40 50 Miles

• County Seat

is appointed to office. Together, the department heads form a group called the cabinet. The cabinet advises the governor and helps run the executive branch.

County Government

Like other states, New Mexico is divided into counties. Today, there are 33 counties. Catron County is the largest in size. Bernalillo County, where Albuquerque is located, has the most people. The smallest is Los Alamos County, formed in 1949. Doña Ana is the fastest growing county.

The county level of government does much to serve people in rural areas. A board of commissioners makes up the executive and legislative branches. The commissioners make laws for the county. They also see that the duties of county government are carried out. A sheriff enforces laws in the county. Another official is the county clerk, who keeps official records.

The county's money is handled by several officials. The job of telling people how much money they owe belongs to the assessor. Then the treasurer takes care of the county's money.

The Colfax County Courthouse at Raton. From buildings like this one, local officials all around New Mexico administer county government. *How does county government differ from state governments?*

commissioners

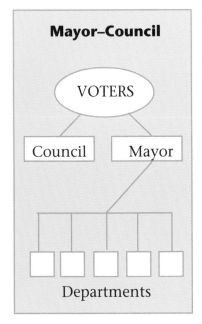

Mayor–Council

VOTERS

Council   Mayor

Departments

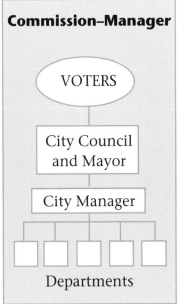

Commission–Manager

VOTERS

City Council and Mayor

City Manager

Departments

municipal

Among other duties, the county collects taxes, holds elections, and repairs county roads. The town where county government has its offices is called the county seat.

Municipal Government

The word municipal refers to local government in cities and towns. A place that has more than 2,500 people is called a city. Places with less than 2,500 people are called towns. The New Mexico legislature gives cities and towns the right to form municipal governments.

As cities and towns grow, these governments must deal with more and more problems. Citizens need daily services. They need police and fire protection. They must have schools and hospitals. Garbage must be collected and streets cleaned. And in New Mexico there is always the question: Where will water for the future come from?

In New Mexico, two forms of municipal government are common. One is the mayor-council form. Here, an elected mayor runs the city. The mayor is helped by an elected council that passes local laws. These laws are known as city ordinances. Albuquerque, Santa Fe, and Las Cruces have a mayor-council form of government.

The second form of municipal government is the commission-manager form. Hobbs and Clovis are cities with this type of government. A commission with five board members runs the city or town. The commission hires a manager, who directs the daily business of the city.

The Bill of Rights

Our government at all levels is supposed to protect and serve the people. In a democracy, individual freedoms are carefully spelled out. A part of the United States Constitution is called the Bill of Rights. It lists the rights of individual citizens. And it keeps Congress from passing laws that take away those rights.

When the New Mexico Constitution was written in 1911, it also had a Bill of Rights. This Bill of Rights was needed to protect our freedoms at the state level. Some of the rights included were civil rights. Among them were freedom of speech and religion and the right of trial by a jury. The state Bill of Rights also included political rights. The right to vote and hold public office are examples of political rights.

Fire protection is one service of city and county governments. This is an early photo of the Las Vegas Fire Department. *What other services do city and county governments provide their residents?*

ordinance
civil rights

Public Education

One of the most important things the state government does is provide free public education. In New Mexico, the State Board of Education watches over the school system. It has fifteen members. Ten are elected and five are appointed by the governor. The Board appoints a Superintendent of Public Instruction to see that its job is done.

New Mexico is divided into 89 school districts. Each district elects a school board that establishes schools and sets policies for them. A superintendent is appointed by the school board to manage the schools. Money to run the public schools comes from the state. Private schools are governed and funded by the groups that own them.

Higher education is offered by colleges and universities. Some are under the direct control of the state. Their policies are set by board members appointed by the governor. Other colleges and universities are privately owned and operated. In New Mexico, young people have a good choice of colleges and universities to attend.

The Criminal Justice System

Crime is a problem in New Mexico, as in every other state. Part of the job of government is to deal with crime. This part of government is called the criminal justice system.

The criminal justice system has become an important part of our government. This system involves the courts, city and county jails, and the state prison. The courts hold trials for persons charged with crimes. Persons who are found guilty of crimes are sent to prison. The purpose of prison is to punish individuals for breaking the law. Also, some criminals are so dangerous that they must be locked away to protect society.

Rows of cells in New Mexico's first state prison.

A good prison system tries to **rehabilitate** as many persons as possible. Rehabilitate means to help prisoners become good citizens. This is done by teaching prisoners new skills and giving them more education. It is hoped that these skills will turn them away from crime. Some prisoners are rehabilitated. Others are not.

In February 1981, there was a major riot at the state prison near Santa Fe. In all, 33 prisoners were killed. Much of the prison was destroyed. It was one of the worst riots

rehabilitate

In primary elections around the state, citizens gather to select party candidates. They also select delegates to national party conventions. *What might these citizens discuss before they choose candidates?*

candidates

in the nation's prison history. This riot happened because of problems in the prison. For one thing, the prison was too crowded. The riot showed that our criminal justice system is not all that it should be. Much needs to be done to make the system better.

Politicians and Parties

A politician is a person who wants to be elected or appointed to a government office. People who share similar ideas about government join together. They form a political party. Members of the party choose **candidates** to run for office. The Democratic and Republican parties are the two leading ones in the United States. Often, smaller parties run candidates for office. But these candidates are seldom elected to office because the smaller parties have fewer members.

The Republicans won most of the elections during much of New Mexico's early history. But in the 1930s, the Democrats became stronger. That was because President Franklin D. Roosevelt, a Democrat, greatly helped the state during the depression. He gained many new voters for his party. Recently, political power in New Mexico has been more evenly divided between the two parties.

In territorial days, many of New Mexico's counties and towns were run by political bosses. A political boss is a person, usually rich, who controls politics behind the scenes. The boss does favors for many people. In turn, they vote the way the boss tells them. By controlling votes, the political boss can help control local and state government.

In early times, some political bosses "voted their sheep." They would give names to each sheep in their flock. On election day, they would cast votes in the names of all their sheep. In one election, there were 4,300 votes in Valencia County. But only 1,800 people lived in the county. Everyone knew that "sheep had voted." Elections are more honest today.

Before elections, candidates put up their signs along streets and highways.

The Indian Pueblo Cultural Center in Albuquerque. *What kinds of activities take place here?*

Indian Tribal Government

Over the years, new forms of government have developed among New Mexico's Indian groups. Slowly, the Indians have won more power in governing their own affairs. Also, Indians are taking a greater part in local and state governments. For example, Navajos have been elected to the state legislature. Members of other tribes serve on local school boards.

Each Pueblo group still governs itself. But the Pueblos also work together. The eight northern *pueblos,* above Santa Fe, have formed one group. They work together in many matters. They also hold a craft fair once a year.

New Mexico's 19 *pueblos* make up the All Indian Pueblo Council. The Council, headed by a chairman, deals directly with the federal and state governments. It speaks with a stronger voice than any one *pueblo* or small group of *pueblos*.

The Council has its offices at the Indian Pueblo Cultural Center in Albuquerque. The Cultural Center is a beautiful building owned by the Pueblo people. Besides the offices, the building contains a fine museum and a craft shop.

The Navajo Nation has one of the strongest tribal councils. An elected tribal president speaks for all the Navajo people. The Navajo also elect 74 council members, both men and women. The Council directs the tribal police and tribal courts. It also handles the many businesses run by the tribe.

Chee Dodge was one of the earliest heads of the Navajo Tribal Council. As a boy, he went on the "Long Walk" to Bosque Redondo. For many years he lived at Crystal, New Mexico. He was a wise person who was much respected. When he died in 1947 at age 87, it was said that "Chee Dodge was a great leader of his people."

Like the Navajo, the Mescalero and Jicarilla Apaches also have councils. These

Chee Dodge, famous Navajo political leader.

Our state is a young one. A majority of our population is under 25 years of age. That is why we must be careful in our decisions to seek long-range benefits for our state. We cannot be thinking of narrow self-interest alone. For this is self-defeating.

—Governor Jerry Apodaca, 1975

councils operate under constitutions, which are written laws of the tribes. One of the most important duties of the Apache councils is to bring jobs to the reservations.

Government for Tomorrow

Government, as we have seen, has many parts. It is always changing, and it touches our lives in many ways. Sometimes government meets the needs of the people. Other times it fails. We must all work to see that government improves.

What does the future hold for our government? We cannot be sure. But we can guess that government will continue to grow. It will be up to us to see that it grows in the right way and does the job it should.

Words to Know

alcalde

candidate

civil rights

commissioners

council

democracy

executive branch

federal

judicial branch

legislative branch

monarchy

municipal

ordinance

politician

rehabilitate

Reviewing What You Have Read

1. What is a democracy?
2. How does a monarchy differ from a democracy?
3. What are the three branches of U.S. government? Tell what each branch does.
4. What are the two forms of municipal government? Explain each form.
5. Which two kinds of rights does our New Mexico Bill of Rights protect?
6. How does our prison system try to rehabilitate prisoners?
7. What are the two leading political parties in New Mexico and the nation?
8. What is a "political boss"?
9. What is the All Indian Pueblo Council? Who was Chee Dodge?

For Thought and Discussion

1. What form of government do you think is best? Why?

2. Why do you think that the U.S. government has three branches? How do these three branches work together? Tell why each is important.

3. In what way do you think that New Mexico government could be made better? Give examples.

Rodeos, fairs, and dances are still much a part of the New Mexico scene. There is more, of course. New celebrations and fiestas spring up with electric excitement and old ones are revived. Fiestas are always in season in New Mexico.

—Statement of the New Mexico Department of Tourism

Giant balloons have become a familiar sight in the New Mexico skies.

12

NEW MEXICO EVENTS

Our world is filled with interesting things to do. We learn by doing. We also have fun by doing different things. In New Mexico, people do all sorts of interesting things in their free time. Our state offers something to everyone.

From Silver City to Hobbs, from Las Cruces to Taos, New Mexicans take part in exciting events. There are all sorts of things to do in our state. Indoors and outdoors, people can have fun and learn at the same time.

Many popular events have their roots in history. They began long ago. Today, such events provide us a link with the past.

These Indian dancers are taking part in the Gallup Ceremonial. *Why are traditional dances important to Indian people?*

fiesta
rodeo

Indian ceremonies, fiestas, fairs, rodeos, and frontier celebrations are part of our early heritage.

Youngsters can often take part in these events. Even just watching is exciting and fun. By playing and working together, New Mexicans gain new respect for their state and its people.

Among the Indians

For centuries, the Indian people held celebrations at special times. The first Spaniards wrote about ceremonies and dances in the plazas of the Pueblos. They described the large crowds that gathered for these events.

At such times, the Indians felt proud of their customs and their people.

That is true to this day. On special days, the Pueblos invite the public to visit them. There may be a beautiful dance or a foot race. Or perhaps it is a time for selling crafts and Indian food. Then, the Pueblos enjoy having guests.

Some events are more serious. These are the religious ceremonies of the Indians. Visitors are often allowed to attend. But they must be quiet and not get in the way. Visitors must show respect, even though they may not understand the ceremony.

Early in December each year, the Zuni Pueblo has its famous Shalako ceremony. The ceremony lasts all night. It is an important religious event for the Zuni.

Most *pueblos* have a **feast day**. This is a special holiday. Catholic services are held in the morning. Indian ceremonies are held later in the day. Usually, the Indians perform a corn dance. Santo Domingo Pueblo has the largest corn dance on its feast day, August 4. Hundreds of men, women, and children take part. It is an event never to be forgotten.

On December 10–12, the Indians of Tortugas celebrate the feast of Our Lady of Guadalupe. Tortugas is a small village south of Las Cruces. Some of these people are related to the Pueblos farther north. During the feast of Guadalupe they walk to the top of a mountain for special ceremonies. Also, dancers in bright costumes perform in the plaza.

August is the time for the Inter-Tribal Indian Ceremonial at Gallup. Indians gather there from all parts of the United States.

feast day

A dancer in front sets fire to Zozobra (Old Man Gloom), opening the Santa Fe Fiesta. *Why is this an appropriate beginning for a fiesta?*

Some even come from Canada and Mexico. This ceremonial is a social event, not a religious one. There are parades, dances, rodeos, and craft shows. Here visitors can see the costumes and customs of many tribes.

Celebrating Our Spanish Heritage

Our Spanish pioneers loved a fiesta. A fiesta was a holiday with church services. But there was much more. During a fiesta, there were dancing, music, games, and horse races. The fiesta was a way to forget the hardships of the frontier.

New Mexico's oldest fiesta is the Fiesta de Santa Fe. It was first held in 1712. The fiesta honored Governor Diego de Vargas and his return to New Mexico after the Pueblo Revolt. For a century or more, the fiesta was not held. Then in 1919, after World War I, Santa Fe citizens started it again.

Now each September, the fiesta brings thousands of people to Santa Fe. On opening night, a giant paper figure called Zozobra is burned. Zozobra is Old Man

Dancers in Bernalillo performing the Matachines Dance, another traditional Spanish celebration.

Gloom. The worries and troubles of the crowd go up in flames with Zozobra. Then everyone can have a good time.

Fiesta events remind us of the early history of Santa Fe and New Mexico. The fiesta begins with a Mass in the old cathedral built by Archbishop Lamy. A religious statue brought to New Mexico in 1625 is carried through the streets. This is the famous statue called La Conquistadora. Men dressed like Governor Vargas and his soldiers march in parades.

In July, the people of the village of Chimayó put on an old Spanish folk play. The play is called *Los Moros y Cristianos*. It is many centuries old. Staged outdoors, the play tells of battles the Spaniards had with their enemies, the Moors. Some of the men dress like Spaniards of long ago. They ride horses, wear steel helmets and capes, and carry swords. Other men dress like the Moors. The play ends with a battle on horseback. There is much shouting and clanking of swords. The people watching clap loudly. *Los Moros y Cristianos* is very popular.

Many towns have celebrations to honor our neighbor, Mexico. Such events usually occur on May 5 and September 16. These days are national holidays in Mexico. Mexican fiestas are held in Las Cruces, Silver City, Albuquerque, and other places.

El Rancho de las Golondrinas

We all know about museums. But do you know what a "living" museum is? It is an idea that has become popular in recent years. A living museum shows life as it once was. The buildings and furnishings of the village or farm are just like those from history. At a living museum we can see how the pioneers lived.

There are a hundred or more living museums in the United States. But only one of these museums tells the story of the Spanish pioneers. It is at El Rancho de las

Golondrinas, south of Santa Fe.

El Rancho de las Golondrinas was a stopping place on El Camino Real. Many famous Spaniards visited there. One was Governor Juan Bautista de Anza. He spent a night at the Rancho in 1780.

Today the Rancho has been rebuilt. The main building is a large adobe house. It has an open *placita* with many rooms around it. In the rooms are things the Spaniards once used, such as furniture, blankets, clay pots, and pans. Next to the main house is a family chapel with a fine bell. Behind the house are barns, corrals, and fields. Old-time mills, which grind wheat and corn, are also there.

El Rancho de las Golondrinas is open to the public through the summer. In June there is a spring festival. In October a harvest festival is held. Thousands of people visit the museum for these festivals. They enjoy learning about history this way. During the school year, children visit the Rancho on tours. They see things they have read about in their history books.

A religious procession at El Rancho de las Golondrinas.

festival

Airplane flights were one of the early attractions at the Territorial Fair. This plane needed a push to get off the ground.

exhibit

Fairs

Fairs have been part of life in New Mexico for centuries. Earlier we learned about the famous Taos Fair. It was the largest fair held during the Spanish colonial period. Large or small, fairs are fun for everyone.

Just about every county in New Mexico has its own fair. People from the county show products of their homes and farms. Horse shows and livestock exhibits are part of the fairs. There are all sorts of other events, too. People of all ages can enjoy music, dances, parades, and carnival rides. Artesia, Lovington, Reserve, Tucumcari, and Springer are among the towns that have well-known county fairs.

There are other kinds of fairs, too. The Northern Navajo Fair at Shiprock includes an Indian *powwow* and rodeo. Arts and crafts fairs are held at Portales, Socorro, and Las Cruces. Roswell's Eastern New Mexico State Fair is a regional fair. People from several counties come to this fair every year.

The biggest fair of all is the New Mexico State Fair. It is held each September at Albuquerque. It grew out of the old Territorial Fair. The beginnings of that fair form an interesting part of our history.

The Territorial Fair

The first Territorial Fair was held in 1881. It took place in Albuquerque because the town was near the center of the territory. Fairgrounds were developed west of the Old Town plaza. The first year, fair exhibits were placed in tents. But a wind and rain storm blew them down. Later, wooden buildings were put up for exhibit halls.

Favorite fair events were horse races, drills by soldiers on horseback, and baseball games. In 1911, a small airplane was shipped to Albuquerque in a railroad car. That year, it flew over the fairgrounds three times as a part of the show. This was the first time most New Mexicans had ever seen a person fly. (Airplanes had only been invented in 1903.) The airplane was the hit of the fair.

powwow

State Fair

In 1912, New Mexico became a state. Then the Territorial Fair became the State Fair. But it did not last long. When World War I came, New Mexicans decided they could no longer spend time and money on fairs. So the State Fair was not held any more.

The fair started again in 1938. At that time a new fairground was chosen. It was on an empty mesa near the University of New Mexico. Cactus and yucca grew there. There were even some rattlesnakes.

Within a few years, however, a fine set of buildings had appeared. They were built in the Pueblo Spanish style. This made New Mexico's fairground different from any other in the United States. Today, it is known as one of the best fairs in the Southwest.

Ballooning

In the last few years, New Mexico has become famous for ballooning. Large colored balloons floating in the blue sky make a beautiful sight. Balloon events are held in towns around the state. The biggest event is Albuquerque's International Balloon Fiesta. It is held each year in October. Balloonists come from all over the world to take part.

Three Albuquerque men made big news

A pageant with a reenactment of Spanish explorers.

with their balloon flight in 1978. The balloon was named the *Double Eagle II*. The men became the first to fly a balloon across the Atlantic Ocean. They landed in France and received a heroes' welcome.

Ballooning in New Mexico is not really new. The first flight was made in 1882! The **balloonist** was Professor Park Van Tassel. In those days, all balloonists were called "professor." Van Tassel's large balloon was named *City of Albuquerque*. It took two days to fill the balloon with gas.

For several years, Van Tassel rode in his balloon at the Territorial Fair. Then he took

balloonist

Most towns in New Mexico have an arena for local rodeos.
Why are rodeos still popular?

it to Hawaii. On a flight over the Pacific, he fell into the ocean. Before help came, Van Tassel was eaten by sharks.

Frontier Celebrations

Many places in New Mexico hold events honoring our frontier past. For example, Lincoln presents its Billy the Kid **Pageant**. Local men and women play the parts of people in the Lincoln County War. Young and old watch history come alive on an outdoor stage.

Alamogordo has a frontier fiesta. Ruidoso puts on mule races. Some years there is a Pony Express race from the town of White Oaks to Lincoln. Española honors our first pioneer, Don Juan de Oñate, with a July fiesta. And at Raton, the Santa Fe Trail Rendezvous is held each June.

The most exciting event carried over from frontier days is the rodeo. Cowboys had to know how to ride bucking horses. They had to rope calves at branding time. Riding and roping have become part of the modern rodeo. These are old skills, long used by the cowboy.

pageant

Rodeos can be found everywhere in New Mexico. Local fairs usually include a rodeo. One of the best is held at Deming during the Southwestern New Mexico State Fair. Cattle towns on New Mexico's plains have very good rodeos. Some of the most exciting rodeos are held by the Navajos and Apaches. These tribes love the danger and challenge that is a part of all rodeos.

A Historic Train Ride

Did you ever want to ride on one of the trains of the Old West? It is still possible to do that. Together, New Mexico and Colorado own the historic Cumbres & Toltec Scenic Railroad. It was once part of the famous Denver & Rio Grande Railroad. Today, the train carries tourists between Chama, New Mexico, and Antonito, Colorado.

Several Hollywood movies have been made using the Cumbres & Toltec. The track passes through high mountains. It crosses bridges, turns curves, and enters long tunnels. Passengers can hear the bell clanging on the engine. They smell the black smoke from

Today, the historic Cumbres and Toltec Scenic Railroad takes tourists through the mountains of northern New Mexico. *Why are people still attracted to the Old West?*

The practice of fast riding through the streets is getting to be a dangerous problem. On every day in the week, but especially on Sunday, the lives of young children and old people are placed in danger by the reckless riding of horsemen through our principal streets. It is time for this useless practice to stop.

—Complaint against horse races in the streets,
   Santa Fe New Mexican, 1868

the coal that runs the trains. They hear the clackity-clack of wheels on the steel rails. All this helps passengers understand what train travel was like long ago.

Farming Festivals

Farming is very important in New Mexico. It provides jobs and brings in money for the state. Farm products are shown at all fairs. Prizes are given for the best products. Some towns, however, have a special farming festival. That festival honors the most important crop in the area.

Have you heard of the Peanut Valley Festival? It takes place each year in Portales. Fields around Portales produce tons of peanuts. The crop is important for the local economy. People at Hillsboro have an Apple Festival. Their orchards produce many bushels of fruit. Visitors to the festival at Hillsboro eat apples and drink apple cider.

Best known is the Chile Festival at Hatch. The rich fields along the Rio Grande grow tasty green and red chile. When the chile is ripe, Hatch has its yearly festival. Events include chile judging, a cooking contest, and hot meals for the thousands of guests. Hatch calls itself the Chile Capital of New Mexico.

Sports and Recreation

Most people love sports. Horseracing is probably the oldest sport still enjoyed in New Mexico. For years, Spaniards and Indians raced their horses wherever a crowd gathered. Now races are held at large tracks in the summer and fall.

Baseball came to New Mexico in the territorial period. An early team was the Albuquerque Browns. This team started in 1880. It played other area teams

One of New Mexico's early baseball teams. *How is this team similar to a baseball team today?*

Deming High School football team in 1913. *How have uniforms and equipment changed?*

Tennis was popular at Kingston in 1888. *What improvements have been made in the game since those early days?*

during the Territorial Fair. Small mining towns had strong teams. The one in Cerrillos was called the Little Pittsburghs. A neighboring team was named the Madrid Blues.

Basketball and football arrived much later. Quickly, they won more fans than baseball. Today, people attend games at their local high schools all across New Mexico. They are eager to cheer for the home team. Games played at state universities draw thousands of people.

Track, tennis, and golf are also popular sports in New Mexico. Nancy Lopez of Roswell is famous. She is one of the leading women golfers in the country. Other New Mexicans stand out as long distance runners.

New Mexico's wilderness areas and lakes offer outdoor recreation. Boating and fishing are popular at Elephant Butte Lake, Navajo Lake, and Conchas Lake. People who enjoy hiking or horseback riding can follow wilderness trails. There are fine ski trails and lodges in several of our major mountain ranges.

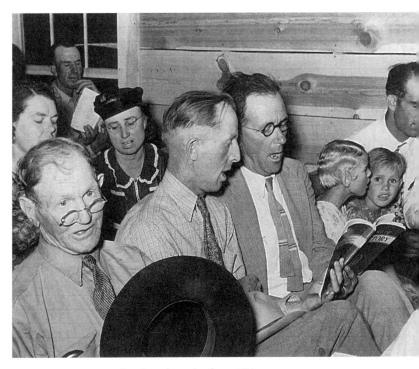

In the days before TV, young and old alike gathered for community singing. *What songs might they have sung?*

Lucky New Mexicans

Sightseeing is perhaps one of the favorite activities of New Mexicans. Our state is filled with exciting places to go and interesting places to see. New Mexico has something for everyone. There are historic towns and places. The land itself is beautiful to see.

Our state is an enchanting land. We are reminded of that by others who come from far away to visit us. Each day we should look around with new eyes. Then we will not forget how lucky we are to live in New Mexico.

New Mexico's Parks and Monuments

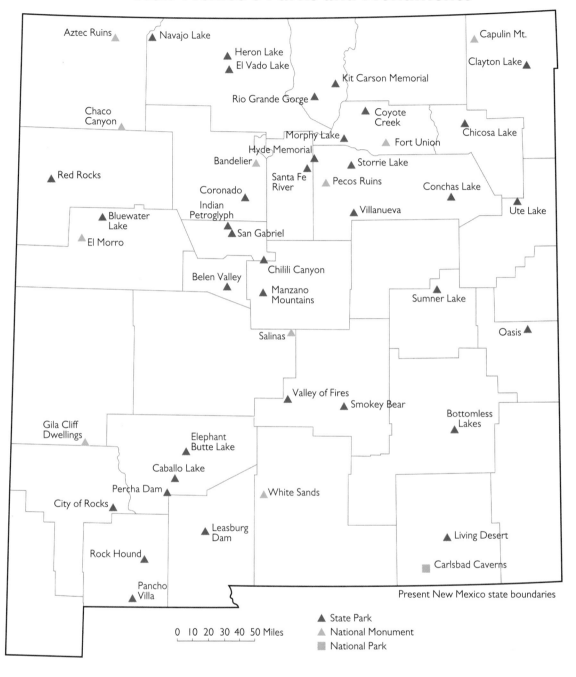

Aztec Ruins

Navajo Lake

Heron Lake

El Vado Lake

Kit Carson Memorial

Capulin Mt.

Clayton Lake

Rio Grande Gorge

Chaco Canyon

Coyote Creek

Morphy Lake

Chicosa Lake

Hyde Memorial

Fort Union

Bandelier

Red Rocks

Santa Fe River

Storrie Lake

Pecos Ruins

Conchas Lake

Coronado

Indian Petroglyph

Villanueva

Ute Lake

Bluewater Lake

San Gabriel

El Morro

Chilili Canyon

Belen Valley

Manzano Mountains

Sumner Lake

Salinas

Oasis

Valley of Fires

Smokey Bear

Gila Cliff Dwellings

Bottomless Lakes

Elephant Butte Lake

Caballo Lake

Percha Dam

White Sands

City of Rocks

Living Desert

Leasburg Dam

Rock Hound

Carlsbad Caverns

Pancho Villa

Present New Mexico state boundaries

0 10 20 30 40 50 Miles

▲ State Park

▲ National Monument

▣ National Park

Words to Know

balloonist	feast day	fiesta	*powwow*
exhibit	festival	pageant	rodeo

Reviewing What You Have Read

1. What is the name of the famous Zuni ceremony held every December?
2. In what city is the Inter-Tribal Indian Ceremonial held each year?
3. Which New Mexican fiesta is held to honor Governor Diego de Vargas?
4. Why is El Rancho de las Golondrinas called a "living museum"?
5. In what city is the New Mexico State Fair held every year?
6. Why did the balloon *Double Eagle II* become famous?
7. What is a rodeo?
8. What crop does the town of Hatch celebrate each year with a festival?
9. Who is Nancy Lopez?
10. Name three very popular boating and fishing places in New Mexico.

For Thought and Discussion

1. Why do you think the Inter-Tribal Indian Ceremonial is important to Indians from all over the United States?

2. In what way can a living museum seem to make the past come alive? What kind of new living museums would you like to see started in New Mexico?

3. How do you think fiestas and festivals help New Mexicans better understand one another? How are such events a part of our culture?

A retablo on
wood by artist
José Rafael
Aragón.

*Swish! Over the logs of the ditch-bridge, where brown water is flowing full.
There below is the pueblo, dried mud like mud-pie houses, all squatting in a
jumble, prepared to crumble into dust and be invisible, dust to dust returning,
earth to earth.*

—Famous English writer, D. H. Lawrence, describing an Indian pueblo
    in the 1920s.

13 CULTURE LEADS THE WAY

Many people have come to New Mexico to look for a better life. They had hopes and dreams. They built their lives here. They mixed with people of other cultures. In doing so, they developed new customs. Over the years, a new culture developed. It is the New Mexico way of life.

At the beginning of this book, we talked about culture. We said that culture is everything created by people. It means a people's way of living. This is the general meaning of the word *culture*.

But we also use the word in a more limited way. In this sense, "culture" means those things that make our lives richer. Art, literature, music, and drama are sorts

literature
drama

This figure of a mountain sheep was placed on a rock many centuries ago. *Where else in New Mexico can you see rock art?*

sculptor
opera
pictograph

of things we call cultural activities.

New Mexico is rich in culture. The three dominant cultures—Indian, Hispano, and Anglo—have all added to it. Today peoples from many different backgrounds also contribute to New Mexico's culture. Artists produce fine paintings. Craft workers make beautiful pottery, weavings, woodcarvings, and ironwork. **Sculptors** shape statues of all kinds. Actors present plays. Musicians perform at symphonies and **operas**. And writers turn out books, magazines, and newspapers.

Let us look more closely at some of New Mexico's cultural activities. These are things that should have special meaning for all of us. They add much to life in New Mexico.

The Artists' World

New Mexico's first artists lived hundreds of years ago. They were Indians who painted on cliffs and boulders. Their paintings are called **pictographs**. Sometimes they had a religious meaning. Indian Petroglyph National Monument on Albuquerque's west side has some 10,000 examples of rock art.

The early Spaniards also painted. Often they painted pictures of the saints on wooden tablets. These were known as *retablos*. Other times they painted religious pictures on buffalo or deer skins. Both *retablos* and skin paintings can be seen in museums today.

The first artists were not full-time artists. They did other things for a living. Only much later did full-time artists appear. They were people who made their living by painting. One was John Mix Stanley. He was a famous American artist who visited New Mexico in 1846. Another was R. H. Kern. He painted scenes at Jemez and Sandia *pueblos* in the 1840s.

Frederic Remington was one of the best-known artists to paint in New Mexico. His paintings of Indians, cowboys, and the U.S. Cavalry became very popular. In 1902, Remington wrote this about New Mexico: "The mountains sweep skyward, range after range—snowcapped, beautiful, overpowering."

Artists came from all over to work in New Mexico. They painted landscapes. Landscapes are pictures of the countryside. They also painted portraits. Portraits are pictures of people, like the Indians and Hispanos who live in New Mexico.

In 1896, American artist Joseph Sharp was in Paris, France. He met two other artists there named Ernest Blumenschein and Bert Phillips. Sharp told them about a visit he

View of Canyon Road, center of the old Santa Fe Art Colony in the 1940s. *Is Canyon Road popular today?*

retablo
landscape
portrait

This painting by Bert Phillips shows young Taos Pueblo women carrying baskets of corn on their heads. *Why was Taos an ideal place for artists to work?*

had made to Taos, New Mexico. The little town, he said, was a wonderful place to paint. One day they should all go there.

The Taos and Santa Fe Art Colonies

Later, Sharp, Blumenschein, and Phillips did move to Taos. They helped start the famous Taos Art Colony. An art colony is a place where many artists come together to live and work. Over the years, one artist after another settled in Taos. Their paintings of Taos Pueblo and the mountains beyond became known around the world.

Many other painters went to Santa Fe. There, another art colony grew up. It was centered on Canyon Road. Members of the Santa Fe Art Colony included Gerald Cassidy, Randall Davey, and John Sloan. Their paintings helped show others that New Mexico was the land of enchantment.

Soon, artists could be found in most of the state's cities and towns. Those in Roswell and Ruidoso painted pictures of the nearby

Hondo Valley. Artists at Silver City did pictures of mountains and ghost towns. Everywhere in New Mexico there were landscapes and people waiting to be painted.

Government Aid for Artists

During the Great Depression of the 1930s, few people had money to buy paintings. Artists could not sell their works. A person who worked for President Roosevelt said, "Artists have to eat like other people." So, the government decided to help.

The federal government gave a lot of money to New

Painter Ernest Blumenschein in his studio. *Do you know the names of other famous artists who have worked in New Mexico?*

Try to appreciate all art. Do not approach a painting with a set formula in your mind as to what it should contain. The painting of the whole world has many points of view. You will obtain great satisfaction by being able to enjoy the art of all races.

—Advice of artist Ernest Blumenschein

The Institute of American Indian Arts.

murals

Mexico during the depression. Part of this money was used to hire artists. They painted large pictures, or **murals**, on public buildings. These beautiful works were painted on the walls of courthouses, libraries, post offices, and universities. Many can still be seen today. The murals are part of the state's art heritage.

An Indian Art School

In 1962, a special art school opened in Santa Fe. It was the Institute of American Indian Art. The purpose of the school was "to open new doors of opportunity" for young Indians interested in art.

The school offered classes in arts and crafts. It also taught music, dancing, drama, and creative writing. Indian students from many tribes around the country have studied there. They saw that New Mexico was a good place to learn about the arts.

The Earliest Writers

Like artists, writers are inspired by the land and people of New Mexico. One of the first writers was Gaspar Pérez de Villagrá. He was a soldier with Oñate in 1598. When he returned to Spain, Pérez de Villagrá wrote a book. It told about his adventures in New Mexico. The book was called *Historia de la Nueva México*.

Later, travelers on the Santa Fe Trail wrote books about their experiences. So did soldiers who fought the Indians, and cowboys who worked on ranches. All these works are part of our frontier literature.

Writer and archaeologist Adolph Bandelier poses for a photograph with his wife.

Fiction Writers

Over the years, many writers of fiction have made New Mexico their home. Fiction works are those made up or imagined by the writer. A novel is a long work of fiction. Short pieces of fiction are called stories. Non-fiction works are based on real-life experiences.

One of the first novels written in New Mexico is *The Delight Makers*. The author was a famous archaeologist named Adolph Bandelier. For many years in the 1880s, he studied the customs of Cochiti Pueblo. In *The Delight Makers,* he told about the ancestors of the Cochití people.

fiction
novel

I'm within an hour of God knows how many different life zones. A half hour in one direction takes me across mesas, down talus slopes, into the Rio Grande Gorge. A half hour in another direction has me in pine forests or in lush mountain meadows through which picturesque trout streams indolently wander. If the chickadees desert my house in April, forty-five minutes up a dirt road brings me back to a cooler habitat they're inhabiting. And who knows how many snowball fights I've had in July, at elevations from which, using binoculars, I can still spot my house down there in Ranchitos, alongside the Pueblo River.

—John Nichols,
If Mountains Die

Frank Waters of Taos is another author who has written about the Indians. He also wrote a novel about Hispano village life. It is called *People of the Valley.* The book tells about the problems some Hispanos have had dealing with the modern world.

In stories and novels, Rudolfo Anaya deals with the same subject. His best-known book is *Bless Me, Ultima.* It tells about growing up in Santa Rosa, a small town in eastern New Mexico.

Judy Blume, formerly of Santa Fe, writes books for young people. Her books are read all over the United States. She knows how to choose subjects that boys and girls find interesting. She writes so that readers feel they are part of the story. What is your favorite Judy Blume book?

John Nichols is another well-known New Mexico writer. He has lived near Taos since 1969. One of his famous books about New Mexico is a novel called *The Milagro Beanfield War.* He has also written a nonfiction book about New Mexico called *If Mountains Die.*

Tony Hillerman's award-winning novels have introduced many readers worldwide to Pueblo, Navajo, and Hopi lifeways.

Nonfiction Writers

Science, history, and nature are some of the subjects used by authors of nonfiction. They write about real-life happenings. One such author was the **naturalist** Ernest Thompson Seton.

A naturalist is a person who studies and writes about wildlife. Seton wrote a popular story about wolves in the Clayton area. It appeared in one of his books called *Wild Animals I Have Known*. He was one of the founders of the Boy Scouts of America. The Seton Museum and Library was built to honor him. It is at the Philmont Scout Ranch near Cimarron.

Mary Austin also wrote about nature. But more often her books describe historical places in the Southwest. One of these books is *Land of Journey's Ending*. It tells about the old customs of New Mexico. For many years in the 1920s and 1930s, Mary Austin lived in an adobe house in Santa Fe.

Writers, as well as artists, find New Mexico a good place to work. More than 150 writers live in Santa Fe alone. Why do you think this is so? What special things about the state cause writers to settle here?

Mary Austin meets a visitor—naturalist Ernest Thompson Seton—at her front door. *Can you name any famous writers living in New Mexico today?*

naturalist

Modern New Mexico wood-workers carve furniture in the old Spanish colonial style. *Why is this furniture style popular today?*

Blacksmiths hammer the hot iron to make beautiful and useful objects. *What were the traditional uses of blacksmithing?*

Craft Workers

Artists and writers led the way to New Mexico. But recently the number of craft workers has increased. Potters, weavers, woodcarvers, metal workers, and others have workshops around the state. They make things that are both beautiful and useful.

Potters shape objects of clay. Some of their pots and bowls are made in the style of the Indians. Others are very modern in form. Today's weavers also borrow from the Indians. A few of them make their own **dyes** from New Mexico plants. For example, cactus fruit gives the color red. A gold color can be made by boiling the bark of an oak tree.

Woodcarving is a very old craft in New Mexico. The Spaniards carved small figures of the saints. They also carved wooden bowls and toys for their children. The village of Córdova is still famous for carving.

This artist is dyeing yarn in tubs and buckets. This method has been used for hundreds of years in New Mexico. *Why do we preserve traditional arts and crafts?*

dyes

One day the priest showed me an old figure of San Angelo, broken. He said, "Pat, do you think it could be fixed?" I said, "Padre, we can try." We worked all night and fixed it. That Santo was done in joints—pieces put in with pipe. I came home and lay on the bed and began to think how you could make it so it would all be in one piece—all one. I could not sleep all night.

Next day, after work, I ate supper quick. Then I went out and got some pieces of wood. I chose some with no knots, and I began carving with my pocketknife.

My wife called to me: "Aren't you going to sleep?" I did not answer her.

—Patrocinio Barela, explaining how he first got interested in carving religious statues

Laura Gilpin, famous photographer of New Mexico Indians.

Patrocinio Barela was a famous woodcarver. He lived in Taos. Although he never went to school, Barela became a fine artist. Many of his carvings can be seen in museums in New Mexico. Museums in other parts of the nation also display his work. Most of Barela's statues have a religious meaning. He often carved saints and other religious figures. Barela died in 1964, at age 62.

Metal workers are now an important part of New Mexico crafts. Silversmiths make fine pieces of jewelry. Tinsmiths produce tin boxes, picture frames, and candleholders. Blacksmiths work in iron. They make many beautiful things, from fire pokers to iron grates.

Photography

Photography is also an art. During the territorial period, photographers traveled all over New Mexico. Ben Wittick, Adam Clark Vroman, and Charles F. Lummis were among these early photographers. They carried large cameras. They tried to record on film the life of the Indian and Hispano people.

Some of our nation's best photographers have lived or worked in New Mexico. Eliot Porter of Tesuque was one. Many of his wonderful photographs look like fine paintings. Ansel Adams of California made several famous photographs of New Mexico landscapes. Laura Gilpin became well-known for her pictures of Indians.

Photographer Ben Wittick with his large view camera. Wittick took many pictures of rural New Mexico 100 years ago. *Is photography popular in New Mexico today?*

Music

Music has always been a part of life and culture in New Mexico. The Indians had drums, flutes, and rattles. At religious ceremonies, men and boys sang together. Be-

Pueblo Indian singers accompanied by drums. *Have you visited any Indian pueblos during celebrations?*

symphony orchestra

fore dawn, an old man often went to the roof of the *pueblo*. He would sing a song to welcome the rising sun.

Music was also important to the Spaniards. The *padres* brought organs for their churches from Mexico. During religious services, the Spanish settlers sang hymns called *alabados*. They sang other kinds of songs during fiestas. They also played music on guitars and violins.

American soldiers entering New Mexico after 1846, brought brass bands. They played marching music and sang patriotic songs. On Sunday afternoons and on the Fourth of July, the bands performed for the public. People gathered in the parks and plazas to listen.

Today, many schools and universities have symphony orchestras. They bring classical music to people of the state. Albuquerque has its own large, professional

A miners' band in an early-day parade at Madrid, a coal town.
How is this parade similar to and different from ones you have seen?

symphony. Santa Fe has its world-famous opera. The operas are performed on an outdoor stage during the summer. An opera is a musical play. Singers act out the story. An orchestra provides music.

Drama

A story told upon the stage is called a drama, or play. Now, with movies and television, plays are no longer as common as they once were. But many people enjoy seeing live actors on a stage. The Albuquerque Little Theater was started in 1930 by Kathryn Kennedy O'Connor. It is the oldest live theater group in the state. Actors from

Culture Leads the Way

The Pueblo-Spanish style of architecture in the 1930s.

New York and Hollywood come to Albuquerque to perform.

Plays are also presented in other New Mexico towns. University theater groups put on plays in such places as Silver City, Las Cruces, Portales, and Las Vegas. They help keep alive an important part of our culture.

Architecture

An architect is a person who decides what a house, church, store, or office building will look like. Will it be beautiful or ugly? That depends upon the skill of the architect. A fine building can be a work of art. The work of an architect is called architecture.

There are many styles of architecture. Most were developed in the Eastern United States or Europe. But New Mexico has one kind that was developed here. It is the Pueblo-Spanish style.

A building of this style looks a bit like an Indian *pueblo*. It also looks a bit like old buildings in Spain. But, of course, buildings are now usually made with modern materials like concrete and steel. However, adobe is being used more and more. The Pueblo-

architecture

Spanish style is a mix of the old and new. John Gaw Meem of Santa Fe was the leading architect of this style.

Libraries and Museums— Centers of Culture

Someone once said, "A good book is the best of friends." We can learn much by reading books. Books can also be fun to read.

Many New Mexicans buy and collect books. They enjoy having their favorite ones always close at hand. However, books can be borrowed from libraries. You have probably visited a public library near you.

Some of our libraries are small. Others are large and have thousands of books. The University of New Mexico Library has over two million books for the use of students. It is the largest library in the state.

New Mexico has some very fine museums. Some are art museums. Others have to do with science, history, and archaeology. The Bradbury Science Hall and Museum is at Los Alamos. More than a half million visitors have seen its science exhibits.

The Museum of New Mexico in Santa Fe has the best historical and art collections. The Albuquerque Museum is one of the finest in the state. Small but good history museums can be found in many New

The seal of the State of New Mexico.

Mexico towns. Some of these are in Roswell, Lovington, Silver City, and Springer.

State Symbols

New Mexico has adopted many different **symbols**. These symbols remind us of our state's rich culture. The best-known symbol is the **Zia** Sun Symbol. It appears in red and gold on our state flag. Red and gold were the official colors of Spain. For the Indians, the Zia sun stood for "perfect friendship." Those words appear in the salute to the state flag:

"I salute the flag of the State of New Mexico, the Zia symbol of perfect friendship among united cultures."

Here are some of our other state symbols:
State flower—the yucca
State tree—the *piñon*
State bird—the roadrunner
State animal—the black bear
State vegetables—the chile and the frijol (bean)
State gem—the turquoise
State fish—the cutthroat trout

symbol
Zia

Everyone should know our state songs. One is *O, Fair New Mexico. It* was written by Elizabeth Garrett of Roswell. She was the daughter of Sheriff Pat Garrett. The other state song is *Así es Nuevo México.* It was written by Amadeo Lucero, in Spanish. Thus, New Mexico has two state songs.

Finally, there is our state seal. It is also a symbol. The seal is used on official government documents. In its center are two eagles. One is the American eagle. The other is the Mexican eagle. Below the eagles is the state motto, written in Latin. The motto is *Crescit Eundo,* or "We grow as we go."

The Value of Culture

Our culture has much to give us. We learn cultural values from our families, friends, and teachers. Through education, we come to understand today's culture. We learn how it works and how we fit in. Together, we all share the culture of New Mexico.

Official State...

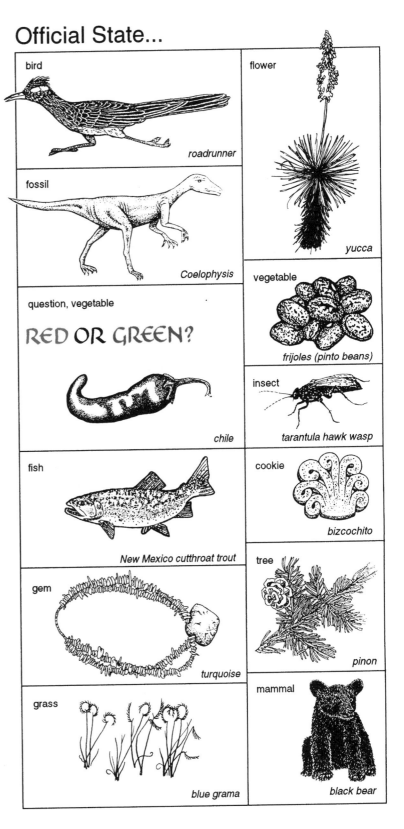

bird — roadrunner

fossil — Coelophysis

question, vegetable — RED OR GREEN? — chile

fish — New Mexico cutthroat trout

gem — turquoise

grass — blue grama

flower — yucca

vegetable — frijoles (pinto beans)

insect — tarantula hawk wasp

cookie — bizcochito

tree — pinon

mammal — black bear

Words to Know

architecture   literature   opera   *retablo*

drama   mural   orchestra   sculptor

dye   naturalist   pictograph   symbol

fiction   novel   portrait   symphony

landscape   Zia

Reviewing What You Have Read

1. Give three examples of cultural activities.
2. What are pictographs?
3. Which famous artist painted pictures of Indians, cowboys, and the U.S. Cavalry?
4. Which famous writer who lived in Santa Fe writes books for young people?
5. What is a naturalist?
6. Who was Patrocinio Barela?
7. Which style of architecture developed in New Mexico?
8. Where is the largest library in New Mexico?
9. What is the state symbol for "perfect friendship"?
10. Give the titles of our two official state songs.

For Thought and Discussion

1. How do cultural activities such as literature and music make our lives richer?

2. Why do you think so many artists came to New Mexico to paint? What was special about New Mexico?

3. Suppose that you are a famous writer. Would you want to write a book about New Mexico? What would that book be about? Why would you want to write it?

14

WE THE PEOPLE

People form a family, community, state, and nation. Society is a group of people working together. The key words are "working together." Without that, there could be no society. There could also be no progress. The people of New Mexico are working together to make our state a better place. People are what makes our society strong.

Our state constitution opens with these words: "We, the people of New Mexico . . . establish this constitution." The power to govern comes from the people. Our country, perhaps more than any other, respects its citizens' rights and talents. New Mexico's people are truly its greatest resource.

History is largely the study of people. As individuals or groups, what we do becomes history. Each of us is interested in knowing what other people are doing. We learn about others today by reading the newspaper, listening to the radio, or watching TV. To learn what people did in the past, we study history.

There are lessons to be learned from history. People and entire nations made mistakes in the past. Knowing this, we can sometimes keep from making the same mistakes. Remember Billy the Kid and Clay Allison? They were New Mexicans whose lives went wrong. Even now, they remind us that violence and dishonesty lead nowhere.

Most people in the past were hard-working and honest. They sometimes made mistakes. But when they did, they tried to correct them. Cowboys said that they liked persons "who kept their word and paid their debts." Such people tried hard and did the best they could.

Which New Mexicans that we have studied do you admire? Would you include names like Manuel Chaves, Marian Russell, George McJunkin, and Kit Carson? In the following pages, we will look at other persons worth knowing about.

A Great Discovery

In 1901, a 19-year-old cowboy named Jim White went looking for lost cattle. He rode his horse into the hills 25 miles southwest of Carlsbad. Suddenly, he saw a strange sight. Millions of bats were flying from a large hole.

Young Jim rode closer. The hole was huge. It was the entrance to a cave leading far down into the earth. Jim wondered what secrets might be hidden in the dark cave.

Several days later, Jim White returned to the cave. This time he brought rope and a lantern. With the rope, he climbed to the bottom of the hole. Using the lantern for light, he followed long tunnels in the ground. Beautiful rock formations were everywhere. Some rang like bells when Jim thumped them. In places, the tunnels opened into giant rooms.

Jim White returned to explore many times. He knew that he had found one of the great wonders of the world. He told people what he had seen in the cave. But few believed him. Some called him the "champion cowboy liar."

Slowly, over the years, others came to see Jim's discovery. At first they named it the "Old Bat Cave." Later, it became known as Carlsbad Caverns. Finally, a scientist visited the cave. He described the caverns as "the

Cowboy Jim White discovered and first explored Carlsbad Caverns. *What might his thoughts have been when he discovered the caverns?*

cavern

One of the rooms in Carlsbad Caverns. Scientists believe it took 60 million years for the Caverns to become as we see them today.

most spectacular wonder in America. It is the King of its kind," he said.

In 1930, the U.S. Congress made Carlsbad Caverns a National Park. Since then, millions of people have enjoyed the place Jim White discovered and explored. One part of the caverns is called the Big Room. It is large enough to hold the Houston Astrodome. Our capitol building in Washington would easily fit into one corner.

Cowboy Jim White never received the honor he should have. Later, others made money from the caverns. But Jim remained poor. Like many of our pioneers, he gave much to the state without a reward.

He was a grand man. Up to this moment justice has not been done to him historically. He discovered the Caverns, in the good old American way of adventuring.

He let himself down with a rope to discover and get acquainted with the unknown.

—Senator Dennis Chávez, speaking of Jim White's discovery of Carlsbad Caverns

Senator Dennis Chávez was one of New Mexico's great politicians of the 20th century. *In what ways was he a model elected official?*

The Politician Who Cared

One person who honored Jim White was Dennis Chávez. He came from a poor family. But Chávez worked hard to become a major figure in our government. When he was elected to Congress in 1930, he promised to be "a good errand boy." By that, Chávez meant he would never forget his duty to serve the people.

In 1935, New Mexico Senator Bronson Cutting was killed in a plane crash. Governor Clyde Tingley appointed Chávez to fill his place. He served as one of our senators in Washington until his death in 1962.

Over the years, Dennis Chávez fought for

justice. He was a leader in the fight against racial discrimination. He helped our country get along better with Latin America. He worked hard to improve rights of the working people.

Though he was an important person, Senator Chávez always had time for the poorest citizen. He remembered that he was one of the people. He never forgot that he was elected to office to serve New Mexico.

Indian Man

Oliver La Farge was born in the East. But he spent much of his life in New Mexico. He worked hard to defend Indian rights. He wrote many books about their culture and problems. In fact, he was sometimes called "Indian Man."

La Farge wrote a book that made him famous. The book was called *Laughing Boy. It* was about modern Navajo life. In 1930, the book won the Pulitzer Prize. That was an important award given to the best novel of the year.

For the last years of his life, La Farge lived in Santa Fe. He was a leader in saving the city's historical buildings. He stood up against those who wanted to make changes without thought for the past.

But mostly, Oliver La Farge worked to help the Indian people. He encouraged the U.S.

Oliver La Farge, author.

racial discrimination

government to return Blue Lake to the Taos Indians. La Farge died in 1963. But he is still remembered as a person who believed in fair treatment for everyone.

Women of New Mexico

So far, we have not said much about women. What part did they play in our history? Why do we not hear more about what women were doing through the centuries?

Women did brave and important things. But often their stories were not written down. What they contributed was forgotten. We should remember, too, that women did not have the same rights as men. Early schools were for boys only. And women could not even vote until the early twentieth century.

In the Indian cultures, women had certain rights. In some tribes, they owned the houses or *tepees*. They also

This young Native American woman and her mother might have certain rights today that they would not have had in earlier times.
Can you name some?

Olive Rush is decorating a ceiling in Las Cruces, 1936.

curandera

had important religious duties. Still, it is clear that men ruled Indian society.

Among the Spaniards, women played no part in business and politics. In wealthy homes, the men of the family ate their meals first. Afterward, the women came to the table and ate. In church, men and boys sat on one side, and women and girls sat on the other.

In Spanish New Mexico, older women sometimes became healers. They were called *curanderas* and took the place of doctors. From her mother, the *curandera* learned how to prepare medicines. She made them from all kinds of plants and other things. When people were sick, they visited the *curandera*. She decided what was wrong and gave them the proper medicine. Her role was a valuable and respected one in Spanish society.

After 1900, women in New Mexico slowly gained more

rights and freedoms. They found new opportunities to take part in life outside the home. Let us look at several women who have made major contributions to modern New Mexico.

Leaders in Their Work

Women have given much to the arts and culture in our state. Georgia O'Keeffe was one of our nation's best modern artists. In 1946, she moved to the village of Abiquiu. Many of her paintings show the mountains and mesas near her home.

Pablita Velarde of Santa Clara Pueblo is another fine artist. Her paintings have been shown in museums around the world. Olive Rush lived for many years in the Santa Fe art colony. During the depression she painted murals all over the state.

Many New Mexico women became fine writers. Archaeologist Florence Ellis has written about the earliest Pueblo people. Fabiola Cabeza de Vaca wrote a well known

Indian artist Pablita Velarde views one of her paintings.

book called *We Fed Them Cactus*. It told about the life of Hispano ranchers on the plains. In the book *No Life for a Lady,* Agnes Morley Cleaveland told about growing up among cowboys west of Socorro.

Erna Fergusson wrote her first book in 1930. Before she died in 1964, she wrote seven more. Her grandfather had come to New Mexico on the Santa Fe Trail. Erna Fergusson spent most of her life in Albuquerque. She knew and loved every part of New Mexico. Her books are some of the best ever written about the state.

"First Lady of Song"

One of the most interesting women in our history was Elizabeth Garrett. She was born blind in Lincoln County in 1885. Her father, Sheriff Pat Garrett, was famous for shooting Billy the Kid.

Life was hard for blind people in those early years. But Elizabeth Garrett studied hard and learned Braille. Braille is a way blind persons can read, by touching raised letters with their fingers. She also loved music. She sang and played the piano.

Elizabeth Garrett wrote music, too. Some of her songs were about the beauty of New Mexico that she could not see. In 1915, she wrote *O, Fair New Mexico!* The next year Governor William McDonald invited her to

Santa Fe. She sang O, *Fair New Mexico!* to the state legislature. It became the official state song.

Elizabeth Garrett was known as New Mexico's "First Lady of Song." She once said: "My father tried to bring peace and harmony to our country with his guns. I would like to do my part with my music."

Individuals with Disabilities

The life of Elizabeth Garrett reminds us of an important fact. The fact is that people with disabilities have much to contribute. They show us what hard work and courage can bring about. The handicapped may need the help of others. But they always have something to give in return.

Long ago, the state started to aid the physically handicapped. In 1887, the New Mexico School for the Deaf opened in Santa Fe. Later, in 1906, the School for the Visually Handicapped was started in Alamogordo. Elizabeth Garrett often visited there. She always brought her seeing-eye dog so it

Elizabeth Garrett with her seeing-eye dog, Teene. *How was she able to succeed?*

Liza Córdova of Albuquerque has represented New Mexico in the International Special Olympics. Here, she poses with Olympic star Bruce Jenner.

could play with the blind students.

Programs for the mentally handicapped came later. A volunteer program to help this group began in 1968. It is called the New Mexico Special Olympics. The program allows children and adults to take part in sports through Special Olympics. The aim in these sports is not to win, but to do one's best. The Special Olympics help the mentally handicapped to gain confidence and new skills.

In Special Olympics it is not the strongest body or most dazzling mind that counts. It is the spirit which overcomes all handicaps. For without this spirit, winning medals is empty. But with it, there is no defeat.

Our greatest respect goes to all who try, who stay in the race, no matter where they finish.

—Eunice Kennedy Shriver,
       sister of President John F. Kennedy

Our Finest Citizens

Life is our most precious gift. We place great value on preserving human life. That is why we have safety programs. Many people in society work hard to save lives. These include doctors, nurses, fire fighters, and the police.

Our greatest praise goes to the person who gives his or her life for another. We see this as the highest act of bravery. Such people inspire us all. They bring honor to our society.

John Braden drove a stagecoach for many years. In 1896, he offered to help with the parade at the Territorial Fair. Braden was given a wagon loaded with fireworks to drive in the parade. Suddenly his wagon caught fire. The horses became frightened and ran through the crowd. They headed straight for a float carrying the fair queen and her court.

Braden might have jumped and saved his life. But he stayed with the flaming wagon. He stopped the horses before they could cause any harm. By this time his clothes were on fire. A few hours later, he died of his burns.

A local newspaper said of him:

"No doubt that John Braden saved the young ladies on the queen's float from death or serious injury. We have never seen or heard of such heroism. He could have jumped from the wagon and saved himself. But he stayed at his post and prevented the horses from killing a number of people."

Two Modern Heroes

Daniel Fernández probably never heard of John Braden. Danny grew up in Los Lunas. He was a serious boy who hoped to be a rancher some day. He joined the army when he was 16 years old.

Three years later, Danny Fernández was killed in Vietnam. He was with four other soldiers. Suddenly a **hand grenade** landed among them. Danny threw his body on the grenade as it blew up. He died instantly. But he had saved the lives of his friends.

In April 1967, the country honored Daniel Fernández. At a White House ceremony, President Lyndon Johnson presented his parents with the Medal of Honor. That is the highest medal that can be given to an American soldier. Two of the men Daniel saved were present at the ceremony. All New Mexicans can be proud of the bravery of Danny Fernández.

Another brave man we should remember is John Baker. He was a track star at Manzano High School in Albuquerque. Later, he won many races for the University of New Mexico. In 1968, John became the physical education coach at Albuquerque's

Specialist Four Daniel Fernández.

hand grenade

Aspen Elementary School. During this time, he started to train for the Olympics in Munich, Germany.

At Aspen, Baker became known as "the coach who cared." He taught each student to do his or her best and never give up. Trying is more important than winning, he often said. The coach was always ready to help when a student had a problem.

John Baker had a serious problem of his own. He learned that he was dying of cancer. There would be no trip to the Olympics for him. Over the next months, John worked even harder for his students. He also served as a coach for the Duke City Dashers, a girls' track team.

On Thanksgiving Day 1970, John Baker died. Two days later, the Dashers won the national track championship at St. Louis. Each girl had run her best for the coach.

Afterward, the name of Aspen Elementary School

John Baker, runner and coach.

A forest ranger, dressed as Smokey Bear, talks to boys and girls about fire prevention.

was changed to John Baker Elementary. The coach's life story was told in a book called A *Shining Season*. That story was filmed and shown on national TV. People around the country learned of John Baker's courage.

The Most Famous New Mexican

New Mexico's best-known citizen was not a person at all. He was a bear named Smokey. As a cub, Smokey was saved from a fire in the Lincoln National Forest near Capitan in 1950. He was sent by airplane to the National Zoo in Washington, D.C.

There, Smokey became our nation's symbol for fire prevention and wildlife conservation. Wearing a ranger hat, Smokey appears on signs outside our National Forests. He warns visitors: "Only You Can Prevent Forest Fires."

Many people have come to think of Smokey as a human being. He receives letters from all over the country. The post office even gave Smokey his own ZIP Code. Youngsters everywhere look upon Smokey as their friend.

Putting It All Together

What do the people (and the bear) in this chapter have in common? You can probably guess the answer. Each one contributed something to New Mexico. Each helped make our state a better place in which to live.

We should all try to do the same. Each of us can find a way to add something important to our family and community. As our state motto says: "We grow as we go." In learning and growing, we do our part for the New Mexico of tomorrow.

Words to Know

caverns   hand grenade

curandera   racial discrimination

Reviewing What You Have Read

1. What famous place did Jim White discover?
2. What did Senator Chávez mean when he said that he wanted to be "a good errand boy"?
3. Why was Oliver La Farge called "Indian Man"
4. In Spanish New Mexico, what was a *curandera*?
5. Why is Georgia O'Keeffe famous?
6. What was unusual about Elizabeth Garrett as a song writer?
7. What did John Braden do to become a hero?
8. Why did Danny Fernández get the Medal of Honor?
9. What two things did John Baker try to get his students to do?
10. Who is our nation's symbol of fire prevention and wildlife conservation?

For Thought and Discussion

1. How can history keep us from making the same mistakes that were made in the past? Give an example of what we can learn from history.

2. Why did women not have the opportunities in the past that they have today?

3. Does a person have to be famous or a hero to contribute to society? Why or why not?

15

LOOKING TO THE FUTURE

This book is about New Mexico's past and present. It is difficult to tell exactly what will happen here in the future. New Mexico's growth and progress bring both blessings and challenges. All New Mexicans must keep informed of the issues and happenings in our state. That way we will stay abreast of the problems that confront us, and we will be able to meet the future with confidence. The best way to prepare for our future is to have a firm grasp on our history.

The new **millennium**, beginning in 2001, is the start of the next thousand years. The close of one millennium and the opening of another causes people to stop and

millennium

think about our past. We remember our history and what we have learned by studying it. This is also a good time to look ahead and get ready for what is to happen in the future.

We are coming to the end of our story. Our trail through history has been a long one. It began with the first Indians who found a home in New Mexico. We learned about the Pueblo people and their culture. Our study showed how the customs of the Pueblo people differed from the customs of the Apache, Navajo, and Ute.

The trail of history led us to the Spaniards. We saw how they explored, conquered, and settled New Mexico. The colonists faced many problems on the frontier. But slowly they established towns, farms, and ranches. They left the strong mark of their Spanish heritage on the land.

The next stage of our story began with the Mexican period in 1821. The first Americans arrived while New Mexico was part of the Republic of Mexico. Some of these Americans were traders who came over the Santa Fe Trail. Others were mountain men who trapped beaver in the southern Rockies.

These earliest Americans prepared the way for conquest. In 1846, General Stephen W. Kearny's army seized New Mexico for the United States. Four years later, a territorial government was set up.

Many important things happened while New Mexico was a territory. The Gadsden Purchase (1853) added land to southern New Mexico. The Civil War brought a short period of bloody fighting. In 1863, western New Mexico was cut away to form the Territory of Arizona. Later, Billy the Kid became a famous outlaw in the Lincoln County War. The territorial period ended with statehood in 1912.

In the twentieth century, New Mexico drew closer to the rest of the nation. Like the other states, it suffered during the Great Depression. It helped defend the nation in two world wars. By the 1940s, the state was becoming a leader in science and space research.

After a study of state government, our story ended with a look at modern New Mexico. We learned about people who have contributed to our state and nation. We saw that each of us has something to offer. Now we should think about the future.

An F-4 Phantom jet slams head-on into a concrete barrier at 480 miles per hour. Sandia National Laboratories does such tests. They help scientists learn more about what happens if an aircraft crashes into important large structures such as a nuclear power plant.

The Hispanic village of Villanueva in the Pecos Valley depends on small farms and livestock for much of its income. *How do you think the future will affect this community?*

New Mexico's mid-sized towns, like Farmington, are growing. New suburbs and mobile home parks are being added. *What are some reasons for the growth?*

The Problem of Progress

Progress means moving forward to a goal. We all hope that our society is progressing. We expect things to improve, to become better and better. But history shows us that progress is not steady. There are periods, such as depressions, when progress slows down and even stops.

With progress comes change. Sometimes change is good. But sometimes it can be bad. For example, years ago, our forests were cut down carelessly. Much damage was done to the environment. But many people said that cutting the forests was a sign of progress. It gave people jobs and provided lumber for houses.

Today, we know how to use the forests without destroying them. Through conservation, young trees are protected and new ones planted. In this case, we have learned how to control progress so that it does not harm the land.

Perhaps you have heard somebody say: "No one can stand in the way of progress!" When you hear that, it usually means change is coming to a neighborhood, a town, or the countryside. It also means that some individuals or groups are going to be hurt by the change.

Our society has learned from the past. But there is still much to know. One thing is how

Timber is one of the state's chief natural resources. In the early days, men cut down thousands of trees. *What is being done to preserve our forests?*

Smokey Bear says: "Keep New Mexico green. Prevent forest fires."

to deal wisely with change. Progress, and its changes, should serve people.

What's Ahead

New Mexico's past is exciting, but its future is exciting, too. No one knows for sure what lies ahead. There are challenges enough for everyone. Knowing history will help us meet some of those challenges. But others will be entirely new. In facing the future, we will have to solve problems unknown to our grandparents.

In years to come, young people will study the history of New Mexico that you helped to make. As you grow up, you will shape the history of our state. Your life and work will be part of that history. What is now the future will someday be the past.

As you look ahead, keep New Mexico's history in mind. It is your heritage and it helps you understand who you are. Our history binds us together as New Mexicans. It is one of the keys to the future.

The Future

To explore strange new worlds, to seek out new civilizations, to boldly go where no man has gone before.
—The mission of the U.S.S. Enterprise, Captain James T. Kirk, commanding

Word to Know

millennium

Reviewing What You Have Read

1. Who were the first New Mexicans?
2. What was the second major culture to come to New Mexico?
3. Why did the first Americans come to New Mexico?
4. In what year did General Kearny occupy New Mexico for the United States?
5. What happened to the New Mexico Territory in 1863?
6. When did New Mexico become a state?
7. In what two areas did New Mexico become a leader in the 1940s?
8. Why is progress not always steady?
9. Years ago, why did many people think that cutting down our forests was a sign of progress?

For Thought and Discussion

1. How did New Mexico draw closer to the rest of the nation in the last century? What events made our state a closer part of the nation?

2. Is progress always good for everybody? Or are some people hurt by the changes that progress brings? What can we do to keep people from being hurt too much by these changes?

3. What contribution would you like to make to New Mexico? How would this contribution help you? How might it help the state?

GLOSSARY

abolitionist   A person who wanted to see slavery ended in the United States.

adobe   Bricks made from sand, clay, and straw.

aerospace   Having to do with airplanes and spacecraft.

alcalde   An official under the Spanish system of government. The *alcalde* was both mayor and judge of a town.

altitude   The height of the land above sea level. A place that has an altitude of 2,000 meters is 2,000 meters above the sea level.

Americanized   To become more like the American way of life; to adopt American ways and customs.

ancestor   A person of the same culture who lived long ago, or a relative who lived long ago.

Anglo   A person in New Mexico who is not Hispanic, Indian, or Black.

antenna   A dish-shaped metal object, or metal wires used to receive radio signals or other kinds of signals.

archaeologist   A person who studies people who lived long ago.

architecture   The way a building is planned and built.

arroyo   A dry stream bed.

artifact   An object made and used by people of long ago. Arrowheads and pottery are examples of Indian artifacts.

astronomy   The study of the stars, planets, and other objects in space. People who study astronomy are called astronomers.

atomic bomb   A bomb whose great power is due to sudden release of energy in the atomic nucleus.

atomic energy Energy that is produced by changes in the nucleus of an atom.

balance of nature A term that describes how plants, animals, and people all depend on one another. When nature is in balance, there is enough food and living space for all.

balloonist A person who rides in a basket beneath a hot air balloon.

blizzard A very heavy snowstorm.

boarding school A school where the students live as well as study.

bolsón A closed valley. Water from streams flows in, but it cannot flow out. The water then dries up in the sun.

boom town A town that suddenly becomes much larger because of some economic activity. Many towns became boom towns when new mines were opened nearby.

border The edge of a state, nation, or territory. On the other side of the border is another state, nation, territory, or place.

burro A small donkey, often used as a pack animal.

cacique A religious leader of the Pueblos during Spanish times. A *cacique* was sometimes also a chief.

candidate A person who is running for political office, or a person who wants to be elected to a political office.

capital A city or town where the main government offices are located.

captive A person who is captured and held by others.

caravan A group of wagons traveling to some far place. People in the wagons traveled together for safety.

caverns Large caves.

census A count made to find out how many people are living in a place.

ceremony A special act or event, often having to do with religion.

cibolero A buffalo hunter in old New Mexico.

civil rights The rights that a person has as a citizen. Freedom of speech is a civil right.

cliff dwellings Homes made under large cliffs by the Anasazi of long ago.

climate The kind of weather a place has from year to year.

code A way of sending secret messages.

colonial period The time in history when New Mexico was a colony of Spain. The colonial period lasted from 1598 to 1821.

colony Land settled by people from another country. That country also rules the colony.

commission A group of government officials formed to handle a special problem or to run a local government.

conquer To take over something, often by force, or to defeat someone or something.

conservation The act of protecting or keeping something from being destroyed or used up.

constitution A written plan for setting up a government; a set of basic rules and laws for running a government.

contribution   The act of giving something, or the thing that is given.

cortes   The congress of Spain, which represented the people.

council   A group of leaders or government officials.

crafts   The making by hand of useful and often beautiful objects such as jewelry, pottery, and woodwork.

culture   Everything created by people, such as beliefs, customs, language, and religion. Culture also means those things that people make or do to express their thoughts and feelings. Art, writing, and music are cultural activities.

curandera   In Spanish times, a woman doctor who helped sick people with herb medicines.

democracy   A system of government in which the people rule themselves by electing their own officials.

depression   A time when the economy is not good. During a depression, many businesses close and many people lose their jobs.

dinosaur   A kind of animal that lived millions of years ago.

drainage basin   Land that is drained by a river.

drama   A play presented by actors on a stage.

drought   A long period of dry weather; lack of rain or water.

dye   Something used to give color to cloth.

economy   All the business and work activity of a nation.

elect   To vote someone into a government office. The candidate who gets the most votes is elected to office.

empire   A large area ruled by a king. An empire usually includes land that was conquered.

environment   All the things around us that affect the way we live and grow.

epidemic   The fast spread of a disease. During an epidemic, many people become ill with the disease.

erosion   The wearing away of the land by water, wind, or ice.

executive branch   The part of a government headed by a governor or by the president.

exhibit   Something that is displayed or shown.

expedition   A group of people who go out to explore.

fandango   A lively Spanish dance.

feast day   A kind of holiday that has religious meaning. A feast day in New Mexico was a time to celebrate a certain saint or event.

federal   Having to do with the national government in Washington.

festival   A large public event held to celebrate some happy occasion, such as a harvest.

fiction   A made-up story, such as a novel or other written work.

fiesta   A Spanish-style festival or public celebration. At a *fiesta,* there is much music, good food to eat, and other activities.

foreman   A person who is in charge of a group of workers.

fossil A trace of an animal or plant that lived long ago. A fossil might be a bone or a footprint of an animal. It might also be the outline of a leaf in mud that has turned to stone.

frontier The edge of a new land just being explored and settled.

fur trapper A person who makes a living by trapping animals for their fur.

geography The study of the way the land is formed, and the plants and animals of the land.

ghost town A town that people have moved away from, leaving only the empty buildings behind.

governor The person who is in charge of a state or territory. The governor is the head of the executive branch of state government.

guided missile A flying weapon that is powered by a jet or rocket motor. The weapon is guided to its target by a person on the ground.

gypsum A white mineral. Sometimes sand is made of gypsum.

hand grenade A small bomb thrown by hand.

heritage All the things and ways that we get from the past.

Hispano A person who has Spanish ancestors, or a New Mexican of the Spanish culture.

hogan A type of house used by the Navajo people.

horno An oven made of adobe and used for baking bread.

independent To be free or not ruled by others.

influenza A disease caused by a virus. This disease once killed many people every year. It is often less serious today because of modern medicines.

interest Money that banks pay to people for letting them use their money for business loans.

invasion An armed attack on someone else's land. The purpose of an invasion is to conquer the land.

irrigation Bringing extra water to the land through ditches, pipes, or canals.

isolated To be alone or cut off from the rest of society. An isolated place is a distant, hard-to-get-to place.

judicial branch The part of government made up of the courts. The Supreme Court is the highest part of our nation's judicial branch of government.

kiva A partly underground building used for religious purposes by the Pueblos.

labor union An organization of workers that tries to get better pay and working conditions for its members.

land grant A method used by the Spanish government to give land to settlers.

landscape The way the land looks to the eye, or a painting of the way the land looks to the eye.

legislative branch The part of the government that makes the laws. Members of the legislative branch are elected by the people to represent them and make proper laws.

life zone A part of the natural environment where certain kinds of plants and animals live. Each life zone has a different climate.

literature   The books and other writings of a culture. Novels, poems, and nonfiction books are all parts of literature.

lumbering   The business of cutting down trees and sawing the trees into timber for building.

mainland   The major part of a body of land. Smaller parts, away from the mainland and separated by water, are called islands.

mano and *metate*   Two stone tools used to grind corn. *Mano* is held in the hand. *Metate* is the stone on which corn is ground.

manta   A blanket woven by the Pueblo Indians.

mesa   A flat table-shaped mountain or hill.

millennium   1,000 years of time. The year 2001 will begin a new millennium.

mission   A kind of settlement started by the Catholic church to bring the Catholic religion to the Indians.

missionary   In Spanish times, a Catholic priest who came to bring Catholic teachings to the Indians.

monarchy   A system of government headed by a king.

municipal   Having to do with city government.

mural   A large painting done on a wall.

National Guard   A kind of army set up by a state.

naturalist   A person who studies and writes about nature.

newcomer   A person who has just arrived in a place.

novel   A long work of fiction, or a long made-up story that is written down.

occupation   The work that a person does to make a living.

occupy   To move in and take control over.

officials   Persons appointed or elected to serve in government.

opera   A kind of musical play. Singers act out the parts and an orchestra provides the music.

orchestra   A group of musicians who play together. An orchestra usually plays classical music rather than popular music.

ordinance   A local law or a city law.

padre   A Catholic priest.

pageant   A play or show put on during a festival or similar event.

pictograph   A drawing made on a cliff or rock by Indians of long ago.

piki   A kind of flat bread made by Indian people.

pioneer   A person who comes to a frontier area to settle and live.

placita   An open patio or space within a house. The term can also be used to mean a small village.

plain   A large area of flat land.

plateau   An area of high, flat land. A plateau is higher than a plain and has a different climate.

playa   A dry lake bed.

politician   A person who is active in politics or in conducting government affairs.

portrait   A painting of a person.

posole   A kind of stew made by the Indians.

powwow   A meeting of Indians for some purpose, often social.

prejudice   A favoring or dislike of a person or thing without good reason.

Pueblo   The name for a group of Indians in the Southwest; also a town or village in the Spanish language. Many Indian towns are called *pueblos*.

racial discrimination   The act of not being fair to people because they are of a different race or culture.

rebozo   A scarf worn by Spanish women.

reconquest   To conquer or defeat again.

rehabilitate   To help a person to change in ways that are socially better.

rendezvous   A meeting place.

representative   A person who acts for someone else.

reptile   A kind of animal, such as a snake, that is cold-blooded. The dinosaurs of long ago were also reptiles.

research   The study of a problem or scientific question.

reservation   Land set aside for Indians to live on.

retablo   A Spanish religious painting done on wood.

revolt   A violent uprising against a government. When people revolt, they want to change the government by force.

revolution   A kind of war within a country fought to change the system of government.

rodeo   A public event where cowboys and cowgirls test their skills against one another.

rural   Having to do with life in the country and in small towns away from the city.

sculptor   A person who makes statues.

shinny   A game like hockey that was popular with children in colonial New Mexico.

sign language   A way that Indians once used to "talk" to those who spoke a different language. The Indians made signs with their hands to show what they wanted to say.

smallpox   A serious disease that once killed many people. This disease has been conquered and wiped out.

solar energy   Energy that comes from the sun.

spacecraft   An object that is sent into space by means of a rocket.

space shuttle   A machine like an airplane that flies into space. It is sent up with a rocket, but it lands on the earth like an airplane.

statehood   The process of becoming a state of the United States.

stocks   Documents that show how much of a company a person owns. To own stock in a company means to own a share of that company.

stress   Pressure on the body or mind.

sunbelt   The warmer parts of the United States, in the southern and southwestern parts of the nation.

superintendent   An official who is in charge of a department or commission.

symbol   Something that stands for another thing.

symphony   An orchestra, or group of musicians, that plays classical music.

tepee   A kind of house used by the Plains Indians. It was like a tent.

telegraph   A way of sending messages by electrical signals through wires. Telegraph messages were a series of dots and dashes (short and long signals), that telegraph operators then put into words.

territory   An area of land that is part of a nation but that is not yet a state.

tewa   A kind of shoe made by the Indians.

tourist   A person who travels to a place for pleasure. The business of helping tourists is called tourism.

trade fair   An event held by a town where people come from all over to buy and sell things.

trader   A person who makes a living by trading or buying and selling things.

treaty   An agreement between two groups of people. For example, a peace treaty tells what both sides agree to do to keep peace with one another.

tricentennial   Relating to an event that happened 300 years before.

tuberculosis   A serious disease of the lungs.

turbine   A machine that uses the wind, or blowing air, as a source of energy. Some turbines look like windmills and work the same way.

uranium   A rare, heavy metal that can be used to make atomic energy.

viceroy   In New Spain, the king's chief representative. The viceroy was in charge and was the top government official.

viga   A large beam of wood used to hold up a roof.

villa   An important Spanish town in New Mexico during the colonial period.

volunteer   A person who joins in a cause to help. Volunteers help because they want to, not because they have to.

wickiup   A kind of house used by the Apaches long ago. It was like a tent and had a frame made from willow poles stuck in the ground.

wilderness   A place where no people live. The natural environment is left as is.

wildlife refuge   A place where wild animals are protected from people. A wildlife refuge is often a wilderness area.

Photograph and Illustration Credits

A key to the photographs on the opening title pages is found in the accompanying Teachers' Manual.

Designed by Emmy Ezzell. Drawings by Katherine Chilton and Noël Chilton. Cartography by Bill Nelson. Typesetting and film preparation by Business Graphics, Inc. Printed and bound by R.R. Donnelly & Sons, Inc. The publisher gratefully acknowledges the gift of color photographs from the archives of Katherine Chilton and John Arango.

Albuquerque Museum, 158, 188, 199

John Arango, i, ii, iii, x, 1, 8, 44, 106, 208, 258, 300

Arizona Historical Society, 62

David Brown, 25

Bureau of Indian Affairs, 36

Annelise Chilton, 17

Katherine Chilton, i, ii, iii, x, 1, 8, 14, 17, 18, 20, 24, 26–27, 31, 45, 46; from *New Mexico Color*, 47; 53, 54, 67, 74, 77, 100, 111, 112, 122, 129, 134, 144, 151, 161, 165, 176, 187, 210–211, 225, 233, 245, 252, 255, 256, 261, 267, 269, 275, 278, 295, 296, 303, 314, 322

Colorado Springs Museum of Art, 91

Mary Córdova, 308

Eastern New Mexico Information Services, 231

Hobson-Huntsinger University Archives, New Mexico State University Library, 200

Los Alamos National Laboratory, 209

Mark Jones Corporation, Santa Fe, 231

Museum of New Mexico, 16 (neg. no. 59167), 28 (neg. no. 48546), 43 (neg. no. 57808), 47 (neg. no. 61660); photo by Alexander Gardner, 48 (neg. no. 2508); 49 (neg. no. 86988), 61 (neg. no. 20206), 65 (neg. no. 42236), 78 (neg. no. 11409), 81 (neg. no. 41984), 83, 87, 97 (neg. no. 7757), 104 (neg. no. 22468), 109 (neg. no. 101496), 113 (neg. no. 38177), 115 (neg. no. 16621); photo by B. Brixner, 117 (neg. no. 12034), 126 (neg. no. 87450), 131 (neg. no. 9896); photo by Dana B. Chase, 132 (neg. no. 11344); 136 (neg. no. 12095.2), 137 (neg. no. 50809), 138 (neg. no. 14095.2), 149 (neg. no. 77640), 153 (neg. no. 50541), 156 (neg. no. 76032), 158 (neg. no. 37917); photo by C. S. Fly, 162 (neg. no. 2115); 170 (neg. no. 71542.1), 173 (neg. no. 50884), 178 (neg. no. 14884), 181 (neg. no. 50413), 184 (neg. no. 4876), 184 (neg. no. 48462), 190 (neg. no. 8640), 192 (neg. no. 13785), 195 (neg. no. 51098), 197 (neg. no. 11708), 202 (neg. no. 66457), 204 (neg. no. 30957), 204 (neg. no. 88941), 207 (neg. no. 71128); photo by T. Harmon Parkhurst, 220 (neg. no. 51397); 223 (neg. no. 87557), 234 (neg. no. 65571), 237 (neg. no. 14667), 249 (neg. no. 73486), 250 (neg. no. 29822), 253 (neg. no. 9866), 264 (neg. no. 36609), 268 (neg. no. 8528), 271 (neg. no. 51145); photo by Russell Lee, 273 (neg. no. 58375); 276 (neg. no. 706), 279 (neg. no. 56432), 280 (neg. no. 19388), 281 (neg. no. 40404), 282 (neg. no. 182), 283 (neg. no. 9128), 285 (neg. no. 14248), 286 (neg. no. 1908), 287 (neg. no. 9178), 288 (neg. no. 30860), 289 (neg. no. 39391); photo by Ernest Knee, 292 (neg. no. 19651); 301 (neg. no 57271), 302 (neg. no. 16741); photo by Ina Sizer Cassidy, 304 (neg. no. 19271); 305 (neg. no. 29280), 307 (neg. no. 57207), 318 (neg. no. 56402), 318 (neg. no. 58283)

New Mexico Department of Development, 185, 198, 290

New Mexico Department of Commerce and Industry, 23, 228, 229

New Mexico State Records Center and Archives, 151; Hubbell Family Papers, 152

New Mexico State Tourist Bureau, 9, 34, 35, 37, 41, 73, 215, 222, 226, 242, 260

New Mexico Tourism and Travel Division, Commerce and Industry Department, 212, 218

Rio Grande Historical Collections, New Mexico State University Library, 171, 272, 317, 320

Marc Simmons Collection, 6, 7, 10, 13, 19, 22; illustration by Betsy James, 32; 38, 40; painting by Gerald Cassidy, 61; 64; drawing by José Cisneros, 66; 68, 69, 76, 85; drawing by José Cisneros, 90; 94, 95, 103; illustrations by Betsy James, 105, 114; 108, 110, 114, 125, 127, 128, 133, 135, 141, 148, 154, 157, 166, 168, 175, 177, 217, 229, 239, 251, 252, 263; painting by Bert Philips, 279; 291, 294, 299, 310, 311, 320

Smithsonian Miscellaneous Collections Vol. 63, No. 10., Pl. 6, 86

Frank Turley, 286

United States Forest Service, Southwestern Region, 312

University of New Mexico Press, 33, 47, 66, 68, 70, 72, 109, 116, 119, 177, 182, 221

University of New Mexico Zimmerman Library, 154

Neil Weinberg, ii

Ben Wittick, courtesy School of American Research Collections in the Museum of New Mexico, 63 (neg. no. 16047), 156 (neg. no. 15783); courtesy Albuquerque Museum, 191

Woodward College, NMSRCA, 271

INDEX